RATIONAL COUNSELING WITH SCHOOL-AGED POPULATIONS: A PRACTICAL GUIDE

❖ ❖ ❖ ❖ ❖ ❖ ❖ ❖ ❖

Jerry Wilde, Ed.S.
Educational Psychologist

East Troy Community Schools
East Troy, Wisconsin

ACCELERATED DEVELOPMENT INC.
Publishers
Muncie   Indiana

RATIONAL COUNSELING WITH SCHOOL-AGED POPULATIONS: A Practical Guide

Copyright 1992 by Accelerated Development Inc.

10 9 8 7 6 5 4 3 2 1

Printed in the United States of America

All rights reserved. No part of this book may be reproduced or transmitted in any form or means, electronic or mechanical, including photocopying, recording, or by an informational storage and retrieval system, without permission in writing from Accelerated Development Inc.

Technical Development: Tanya Benn
Virginia Cooper
Cynthia Long
Marguerite Mader
Sheila Sheward

Library of Congress Cataloging-in-Publication Data

   Wilde, Jerry, 1962-
     Rational counseling with school aged populations : a practical guide / Jerry Wilde.
      p.   cm.
     Includes bibliographical references and index.
     ISBN 1-55959-040-8
     1. Rational-emotive psychotherapy.   2. Child psychotherapy.
   3. Adolescent psychotherapy.   4. Counseling in elementary education.
   5. Counseling in secondary education.   I. Title.
   RJ505.R33W55   1992
   618.92'8914--dc20   92-53190
                                                               CIP

LCN: 92-53190
ISBN: 1-55959-040-8

Order additional copies from:

**ACCELERATED DEVELOPMENT INC.
PUBLISHERS**
3808 West Kilgore Avenue
Muncie, Indiana 47304-4896
Toll Free Order Number 1-800-222-1166

FOREWORD

Soon after I started practicing rational-emotive therapy (RET) in January 1955, I saw that it could be successfully applied to children. Because many of my clients spontaneously began teaching the ABCs of RET to their own children, four years and older, they said that it often worked very well and helped the children—as well as their parents—with their emotional and behavioral problems. So in 1966 I, along with Janet Wolfe and Sandra Moseley, published *How to Raise an Emotionally Healthy, Happy Child* (Ellis, Mosely, & Wolfe, 1966) and it has been in print ever since.

Still experimenting in using RET with children, the Institute for Rational-Emotive Therapy in New York started The Living School in 1971 and kept it going for five years—to prove, which we did, that teachers, under the guidance of psychologists (Bill Knaus and myself) could teach RET to their pupils during everyday classroom activities. Out of this project came Bill's pioneering book, *Rational Emotive Education* (Knaus, 1974), Gerald and Eyman's (1981) *Thinking Straight and Talking Sense: An Emotional Education Program*, and my article "Rational-Emotive Guidance" (Ellis, 1978).

These early books were later followed by a number of other books and articles on rational-emotive education and parenting—especially, Ellis and Bernard (1983), *Rational-Emotive Approaches to the Problems of Children;* Bernard and Joyce (1984), *Rational-Emotive Therapy with Children and Adolescents;* and Vernon (1989), *Thinking, Feeling and Behaving.* Jerry Wilde, the author of the present book, also brought out one of the first RET games, which we have found to be quite useful in teaching RET to youngsters. Finally, when cognitive-

Foreword   iii

behavior therapy followed RET in the 1960s, a number of closely related books and articles on using it with children were published, such as Kendall and Braswell (1984), *Cognitive Behavioral Therapy for Impulsive Children.*

All of the above works are useful and Jerry Wilde, in *Rational Counseling with School-Age Populations: A Practical Guide,* mentions and uses a number of them. His book, however, is somewhat unique in that it is written for school counselors and in real detail shows them how to use the theory and practice of RET in their work with younger and older children. Jerry has an excellent background in and understanding of RET and has applied it for a number of years to young people. He stresses its ABC's and how they can be taught to and used by children. But he also sees that RET is always emotive and behavioral and is multifaceted in its methods.

Because children have cognitive limitations, Jerry shows that RET had better be especially adapted so that they can understand and use it successfully. His counseling manner, moreover, is unusually friendly and noncondescending and is considerably helpful in this respect with the pupils that he counsels and with whom he seems to get great rapport.

Jerry's book is replete with many conversational examples of how he uses RET with his child population; and it includes a good part of several sessions with one child. I find his verbatim conversations charming and instructive; and although other counselors, teachers, and parents need not mimic his style, I am sure that many of them will learn considerably from it.

On the whole, this is a simple but solid book on the use of RET with young people and I am quite happy to see it added to the RET armamentarium of methods of working with children and adolescents who have emotional and behavioral problems. Read it—and benefit and enjoy!

March 1992

Albert Ellis, Ph.D., President
Institute for Rational-Emotive Therapy
45 East 65th Street
New York, NY 10021

Rational Counseling With School Aged Populations

REFERENCES

Bernard, M.E., & Joyce, M.R. (1984). *Rational-emotive therapy with children and adolescents.* New York: Wiley.

Ellis, A. (1978). Rational-emotive guidance. In E.I. Arnold (Ed.), *Helping parents with their children.* New York: Brunner/Mazel.

Ellis, A., & Bernard, M.E. (Eds.). (1983). *Rational-emotive approaches to the problems of childhood.* New York: Plenum.

Ellis, A., Moseley, S., & Wolfe, J.L. (1966). *How to raise an emotionally healthy, happy child.* North Hollywood, CA: Wilshire.

Gerald, M., & Eyman, W. (1981). *Thinking straight and talking sense: An emotional education program.* New York: Institute for Rational-Emotive Therapy.

Kendall, P.C., & Braswell, L. (1984). *Cognitive behavioral therapy for impulsive children.* New York: Guilford.

Knaus, W. (1974). *Rational emotive education.* New York: Institute for Rational-Emotive Therapy.

Vernon, A. (1989). *Thinking, feeling, behaving: An emotional education curriculum for children.* Champaign, IL: Research Press.

vi   Rational Counseling With School Aged Populations

ACKNOWLEDGEMENTS

I would like to thank Polly, my wife, for the many hours of typing, tremendous support and encouragement. Thanks also goes to my brother, John, for reasons too numerous to mention. Mosh, Spazmo, and Herb (the wonder cats) are deeply appreciated for their comic relief. Without the chance to work with Dr. George Harper I would be ignorant to the beauty of RET. Thanks, George! My deepest respect, admiration, and thanks go to all the doctors and nurses at Froedtert Memorial Lutheran Hospital for keeping me alive long enough to write this book. This book is dedicated to the children and to the professionals who spend their lives trying to help.

viii   Rational Counseling With School Aged Populations

PREFACE

The idea for writing a practical guide for the use of Rational-Emotive Therapy (RET) with school aged children and adolescents came from numerous discussions with mental health professionals. Many of my collegues seemed to recognize the term RET and undoubtedly had been exposed briefly to this school of psychotherapy in either academia or through professional contacts. However, most of my collegues had retained only a basic, overly simplistic understanding of the model and did not comprehend the true possibilities of this system known as RET.

Today, in America, we face a crisis in our schools not the least of which is the ever increasing number of seriously disturbed children. This book is for those of you who work with this population. What I've heard time and time again from my friends and collegues is that they are frustrated with the type of therapy they are currently using. An extremely disheartening experience is to realize that after hours of therapy no lasting change has occurred in the client. They realize something is missing and are looking for a new approach . . . "something that works." Hopefully, this book will be the first step on that new path.

Throughout this book a detailed analysis of RET will be presented. Fundamental principles such as the A,B,C model of problem identification and resolution will be focused upon. The primary emphasis is on specific techniques to be used with specific problems. Numerous case examples are provided to help illustrate important points.

Preface   ix

The latter portion of the book has been addressed to problems commonly occurring in childhood and adolescent years. Depression, anxiety, anger, low frustration tolerance, low self-esteem, and alcohol/drug addiction are discussed. Considerations and suggestion for individuals interested in working with clients in group therapy using the principles of RET also are presented.

CONTENTS

FOREWORD .... **iii**

References .... *v*

ACKNOWLEDGEMENTS .... **vii**

PREFACE .... **ix**

LIST OF FIGURES .... **xvi**

RATIONAL THINKING THROUGHOUT THE AGES 1

1 INTRODUCTION **3**

2 DEVELOPMENT OF RATIONAL-EMOTIVE THERAPY **5**

3 THEORY OF RATIONAL-EMOTIVE THERAPY **7**

Irrational Beliefs *11*

Philosophy of Rational-Emotive Therapy *14*

4 WHY USE RATIONAL-EMOTIVE THERAPY? **19**

When Doesn't RET Work? *22*

5 THE PRACTICE OF RET **25**

Initial Considerations *25*

Referred and Self-referral *27*

Rapport *28*

Assessment *30*

    Tape and Worksheet *33*

    Feeling Thermometer *34*

    Rational Sentence Completion Task *34*

    Play Therapy *34*

    Checklists *35*

The ABC's of RET *36*

Table of Contents   *xi*

Rational Versus Irrational 42
Rational Emotive Imagery (REI) 44
Disputation 46
    Behavioral Disputations 50
    Emotive Disputations 51

6 DEPRESSION 55

Case Example 55
Berating Self 56
Correlates of Irrational Beliefs 56
Overgeneralization 57
Personalizing Experiences 58
Embracing the Negative 58
Techniques 59
    Bad 100% Technique 59
    Challenge the C Technique 61
    Flat Tire Technique 61
    Eliminate the Irrational Technique 61
    Breaking the Cycle Technique 62

7 SELF-ESTEEM 65

Love Slobs 68
Intervention Technique 69

8 ANXIETY 71

Ways of Distorting Anxiety 72
Discomfort Anxiety 72
Behavioral Techniques 75
    Token Reinforcement Technique 75
    Emotive Technique 75
    Prescribing the Symptom Technique 76
    Rational-Emotive Imagery Technique 77
    Assuming Worse Anxieties Are Realized Technique 77

9 ANGER 79

Techniques 80
    Disputing Irrational Commandment Technique 80
    Attacking Musturbating Technique 81
    Give Up Your Anger Technique 82
    Losing My Temper Technique 82

10 LOW FRUSTRATION TOLERANCE 85

Techniques for LFT 87
    Disputation Technique 87
    Forceful Dialogue Technique 88
    Parameter Establishment (Timer) Technique 88

Underachievement Techniques 89
    Targeting and Disputing Beliefs Technique 89
    Time Parameter Technique 90
    Behavioral Contract Technique 90
    Cognitive Self-talk Technique 90

11   ALCOHOL AND DRUG ADDICTION 91

Treatment and Techniques 93
    Problem Identification 94
    Challenging the Logic Technique 95
    Goal Setting Technique 95
    Assessment Technique 95
    Differentiating Between Want and Need Technique 97
    Recognizing Choice Exists Technique 98
    Stopping Self-downing Technique 99
    Examining Triggers Technique 100
    Breaking Away from a Peer Group 101
    Waiting for the Want Technique 101

12   RATIONAL-EMOTIVE THERAPY IN GROUPS 103

Organizational Structure 103
    Homogeneous Versus Heterogeneous Grouping 103
    Number and Length of Sessions 104
    Group Size 104
    Closed Versus Open Group 104
    Therapist Versus Co-therapist 104
    Group Leadership 105
    Rules 105
    Contract 106
    Student Solution 106
    Retaining Versus Expelling a Member 106
Assessment Techniques 107
    Scenario Technique 107
    Rational Sentence Completion Task Technique 107
    Use of Inventory and Survey Technique 108
Homework 108
Special Problems in Groups 110
    Unequal Participation (Wessler & Wessler, 1980) 110
    Off Task Behavior 111
    Advice Getting (Wessler & Wessler, 1980) 111
Sample Lessons 111
    Lesson 1: Welcome to the Group 112
    Lesson 2: Feeling Words 112
    Lesson 3: Thoughts and Feelings 113
    Lesson 4: Rational versus Irrational 114
    Lesson 5: Anger 116
    Lesson 6: Disputing 116
    Lesson 7: Rating 117
    Other Lessons 118
Let's Get Rational (LGR) 118

13 RATIONAL-EMOTIVE THERAPY WITH PARENTS 123

Beliefs *125*
   Beliefs That Lead to Depression *125*
   Beliefs That Lead to Self-Blame and Pity *125*
   Beliefs That Lead to Anger *126*
   Beliefs That Lead to Anxiety *126*
   Beliefs That Lead to Upset in General *127*
   Beliefs That Lead to Guilt *127*
Assessment *128*
Insights for Parents *129*
   Insight #1 .... *129*
   Insight #2 .... *129*
   Insight #3 .... *130*
   Insight #4 .... *130*
   Insight #5 .... *130*
Overcoming Problems *131*
   Overcoming Problems with Hostility *131*
   Overcoming Fears *132*
   Overcoming Achievement Difficulties *133*

14 RATIONAL-EMOTIVE THERAPY WITH TEACHERS   135

Structure *136*
Value of RET for Teachers *137*
Common Irrational Beliefs of Teachers *138*
   I'm Terrible *138*
   Children Must Be Different *139*
   Things Are Awful *140*
Approaches and Outcomes *141*

15 TRANSCRIPTION 143

Transcript of Interview with Maria *143*
   Author's Notes *149*
   Session 2 .... *150*
   Author's Notes *152*
   Session 3 .... *152*
   Author's Notes *155*

16 FINAL NOTES 157

APPENDIX 159

Figure 1 Rational Sentence Completion Task *161*
Figure 2 Children's Survey of Rational Beliefs: Form B, Ages 7-10 .... *163*
Figure 3 Children's Survey of Rational Beliefs: Form C, Ages 10-13 .... *167*
Figure 4 Answer key to the Children's Survey
   of Rational Beliefs for Forms B and C *175*
Figure 5 The Idea Inventory *177*

BIBLIOGRAPHY **181**

INDEX **189**

ABOUT THE AUTHOR **197**

LIST OF FIGURES

Contents

6.1 A technique to remind children not to confuse their behavior with their "value as a person." 60

12.1 Happening—Thought—Feeling— Behavior Diagram 113

Appendix

1 Rational Sentence Completion Test 161

2 Children's Survey of Rational Beliefs: Form B, Ages 7-10 163

3 Children's Survey of Rational Beliefs: Form C, Ages 10-13 167

4 Answer key to the Children's Survey of Rational Beliefs for Forms B and C 175

5 The Idea Inventory 177

RATIONAL THINKING
THROUGHOUT THE AGES

"Men are not disturbed by things, but by the views they take of them."

Epictetus

"If thou art pained by an external thing, it is not this thing that pains thee, but thy own judgment about it. And it is in thy power to wipe out this judgment now."

Marcus Aurelius

"There's nothing either good or bad but thinking makes it so."

William Shakespeare

"As you think, so shall ye be."

Jesus Christ

"I saw that all things I feared, and which feared me, had nothing good or bad in them save in so far as the mind was affected by them."

Spinoza

"We become what we think about all day long."

Ralph Waldo Emerson

"People are about as happy as they make their mind up to be."

Abraham Lincoln

"Change your thoughts and change your world."

Norman Vincent Peale

2   Rational Counseling With School Aged Populations

CHAPTER **1**

INTRODUCTION

A fourteen-year-old female (Maria) arrives at your office. She has been referred to you by her social studies teacher. What background information you do have is sketchy. From what you do know, the case appears to be that this child's family is having some serious difficulties.

The young lady seems tense. She sits with her legs and arms crossed and stares at the floor. When she does look up, she does so only for a brief glance before staring back down at her lap. While she is obviously upset she does appear to be willing to spend some time talking to you.

From what the child says she lives at home with her mother, father, and two brothers. The parents had previously been separated and have been arguing a lot as of late. Her father, who appears to have an explosive temper, blames the daughter for most of the family difficulties and states *"if you wouldn't be such a little bitch, things would be a lot better around here."* Up to this point he has not physically assaulted anyone, but he does verbally abuse them on nearly a daily basis.

After twenty-five minutes, what is apparent is that Maria is suffering from intense anxiety that is not only a problem when she is in the company of her father. Growing up in a home where predicting her father's behavior is nearly impossible has left her feeling as if she can not cope with

Ch 1   Introduction   3

even the simplest of social situations. She gets frequent headaches and claims that she usually does not sleep well.

Some indications are that she may have low self-esteem. Her lack of eye contact, the way she physically cowers, and her body language all suggest that Maria does not have a high opinion of herself. A legitimate concern is that she may be depressed. She claims to be losing weight because she is not eating, has little or no energy, and spontaneously breaks into tears. A child who is told that he/she is *"fat, stupid, and no damn good"* will eventually incorporate these beliefs into own view of self.

At this point I might tell you that this is a real child and the information I've presented so far is authentic. I did meet with her father and encouraged him to get the entire family into therapy. I even put him on the phone with a local mental health agency so he could make an appointment from my office but like so many of our dysfunctional families, they failed to attend even one session.

This is exactly the type of case that used to frustrate me to no end. How do we help these children with problems that appear to be beyond their control? We can be good listeners and support these children for an hour a week but what lasting good will that do? That's like putting a band-aid on a severed artery. How do we "arm" these children with skills that will allow them to cope with similar situations later in adolescence and into their adult lives?

KEEP READING AND I'LL TELL YOU!!!

Throughout this book I am going to try to clearly explain the theory, philosophy, and specific techniques used to deal with common problems associated with childhood and adolescence using a remarkable system of psychotherapy known as Rational-Emotive Therapy (RET). This cognitive-behavioral school of therapy encourages analysis and alteration of a client's basic philosophical beliefs as a means to emotional and behavioral change. While this book primarily focuses on specific techniques to be used with specific problems, the following chapters present a brief background regarding the development, philosophy, and theory of RET.

CHAPTER **2**

DEVELOPMENT OF RATIONAL-EMOTIVE THERAPY

The originator of RET is Albert Ellis, a psychologist who received his doctoral degree from Columbia University in 1947 (Bernard & DiGuiseppe, 1990). Ellis began his career as a classical psychoanalyst but became dissatisfied with analysis as a means of treatment. As Ellis has said on several occasions, he believes he was born with a "gene for efficiency" and found traditional analysis quite inefficient for several reasons:

1. Many clients stayed in therapy for a considerable period of time.

2. Even after a client would appear to understand an apparent conflict that was causing his/her difficulties, the person would continue to act in the same disturbed manner (Ellis, 1962).

3. While some clients improved, very few were cured.

During the spring of 1955, Ellis had begun to use new techniques. When working with his clients, he began to practice face-to-face psychoanalysis. He felt this was an improvement over traditional psychoanalysis with the patient on a couch and the therapist in a chair at the head of the couch. Ellis

Ch 2   Development of Rational-Emotive Therapy   5

(1962) commented, "Much to my surprise, this more superficial method actually started to produce not only quicker but apparently deeper and more lasting effects." (p.8)

However, many of the problems that plagued traditional analysis were also a problem with this neo-analysis (see above).

Ellis (1985) claimed that he developed the principles of RET working on his own problems such as fear of approaching females and of speaking in public. Ellis sought out situations to face his anxieties, even though he felt quite uncomfortable. He found that once he faced his anxieties they quickly disappeared.

At this point, Ellis began calling his new form of psychotherapy Rational Therapy. The name was subsequently changed to Rational-Emotive Therapy to avoid the incorrect association with an 18th century philosophical approach known as rationalism which it opposes.

Despite considerable opposition and misunderstanding, Ellis has continued to teach, practice, write about, and adapt RET for the past 37 years. Today, RET is reported to be one of the world's most popular forms of therapy (Heesacker, Hepner, & Rogers, 1982). Authors of that study performed a frequency analysis of over 14,000 references appearing in journals between the years 1980 and 1981. Ellis was the most frequently cited author after 1957. Ellis has contributed over 50 books and monographs selling over 6,000,000 copies and continues to work to refine and improve RET (Bernard & DiGuiseppe, 1990).

CHAPTER **3**

THEORY OF RATIONAL-EMOTIVE THERAPY

As stated earlier, the basic underlying principle of RET is that people are disturbed by their view of events, not by events themselves. In other words, **WE FEEL HOW WE THINK.** For example, if 100 children received a failing grade on their report card, would they all experience the same emotional response? Of course not . . . a range of emotions would occur with some feeling depressed, some angry, and even some indifferent.

What produces these different emotions? Logically if an event (failing) causes the emotions, individuals having had the same experiences will have the same feelings. Since we have already pointed out that this is not the case, clearly the emotions must be produced by something other than an event such as failing. That "something" is the individuals' beliefs, thoughts, and ideas about failing. In other words, how we think ABOUT the event is what actually determines how we feel about the event.

For example, an individual who is depressed regarding the failing of a class would probably be thinking something along these lines: Belief Leading to Depression—"*What a worthless person I am because I failed. This proves I am absolutely no good.*"

Ch 3   Theory of Rational-Emotive Therapy   7

An individual feeling angry regarding the failure would probably be thinking something like this: Belief Leading to Anger—"*I shouldn't have failed. It is not fair! That teacher is a rotten person who should be made to pay.*"

A person who has failed might even be indifferent by thinking the following: Belief Leading to Indifference—"*This class is totally irrelevant and I could care less what grade I get.*"

One of our uniquely human abilities is our capability to "think about our thinking." This self-talk or internal dialogue goes on nearly all the time but often times is unnoticed. I like to think of it like breathing . . . it goes on 'all the time and we are usually not aware of it. However, when we are conscious of it we can modify our self-talk in any number of ways.

If our beliefs cause the emotions, we feel then WE CAN CHANGE HOW WE FEEL BY CHANGING HOW WE THINK. This is obviously easier said than done, but hopefully by the time you finish this book, you'll have some skills that will allow you to help your clients do just that.

The goals of RET then can be summarized as follows:

1. To make the child more aware of his/her self-talk and internal dialogue so he/she will be able to think more rationally, clearly, and logically.

2. Teach the child to evaluate own thinking in hopes of allowing him/her to feel more appropriate feelings and fewer disturbed emotions.

3. Teach the child the skills to use Rational-Emotive principles so he/she will act more functionally and be better able to achieve own goals in life. (Ellis & Bernard, 1985).

The core of disturbed behavior is typically found in people's tendency to take their strong preferences for success, approval, and comfort and turn them into absolute necessities (Bernard

8   Rational Counseling With School Aged Populations

& DiGuiseppe, 1990). This is what Ellis is referring to when he discusses the **tyranny of the shoulds.** A child may hold the rational belief, *"I want to get a good grade on my science test."* Many times a part is added that makes the belief irrational. Such beliefs may look like this: *"I want to get a good grade and therefore I HAVE TO GET A GOOD GRADE!"* which will probably create a fair amount of anxiety.

A teenager who believes others must treat him/her fairly will be angry and vindictive when others do not treat him/her fairly, which is bound to happen from time to time. Such demands are easily and often ignored by others.

A five year old who believes that he/she must continually receive praise from his/her parents in order to feel comfortable will be insecure due to their inability to meet his/her neurotic needs!

Ellis has stated that he believes humans have a biological tendency to think irrationally and distort reality such as this. Apparently nearly everyone has this tendency to take a desire and turn it into a demand; therefore, Ellis has concluded that doing so is most likely a tendency inborn in man.

How do you, the therapist, distinguish between rational and irrational beliefs? This is a question that can not be answered with a paragraph. A helpful rule of thumb has been provided by Walen, DiGuiseppe, and Wessler (1980) who stated that anything that promotes survival and happiness can be defined as rational. If you can remain cognizant of that criteria, probably you will not be too far off track in your dealings with clients.

A 16-year-old girl who was referred to me by her parents who explained the she was having a "nervous breakdown." The girl was a perfect 4.0 grade point average, class treasurer, sang in the choir, and worked after school. She excelled in everything she attempted but also had ulcers. The fact that she was an achiever did not change the fact that she was paying a heavy price for her successes.

Ch 3   Theory of Rational-Emotive Therapy   9

After two sessions we had narrowed in on her irrational self-talk which was something like,*"I have to be perfect at everything I do or it proves I'm no good."* Ask yourself, rational or irrational? Is this a wish or a demand? Is it relative or absolute? Finally, is it leading to happiness or preventing happiness?

Obviously, this belief is highly irrational and as a rule you can rest assured anytime you find a human (who is fallible) trying to be perfect, eventually he/she will have serious emotional pain. This thinking will eventually break a person down. Perfectionism has its advantages but it is still a sickness. Eventually it will lead to much more pain and misery than all the successes are ever worth.

At this point going over a few more rules of thumb may be helpful to be used when trying to determine whether or not a belief is rational or irrational. Walen, DiGuiseppe, and Wessler (1980) provided these helpful reminders:

RATIONAL BELIEFS

- are true
- can be supported by evidence or proof
- are logical
- are NOT absolute commands
- are desires, wishes, hopes, and preferences
- produce moderate emotions such as sadness, irritation, and concern
- help you reach your goals

IRRATIONAL BELIEFS

- are false
- lead to inaccurate deductions
- often are overgeneralizations
- are commands, shoulds, and needs
- lead to disturbed emotions such as depression, rage, and anxiety
- hinders you from reaching your goals

Rational Counseling With School Aged Populations

IRRATIONAL BELIEFS

Ellis (1977) detailed the 12 major irrational beliefs. These 12 irrational beliefs with summary information is provided in the paragraphs that follow.

The idea that you must-yes, must-have sincere love and approval almost all the time from all the people you find significant.

Such a belief is not only unrealistic and unobtainable but also is the type of belief that allows a person to waste a good deal of valuable time and energy trying to win everyone's approval. RET holds that others' approval and love are nice but not a need to survive. Additionally, an individual who believes this belief is at danger of not looking after his/her own best interests. Such persons are so anxious to please other people that they seldom take care that their own desires get met.

The idea that you must prove yourself thoroughly competent, adequate, and achieving; or that you must at least have real competence or talent at something important.

Again, RET does not rate competence as a need, only as a preference. This belief leads to self-rating and eventually self-downing which has many negative consequences.

The idea that people that harm you or commit misdeeds rate as generally bad, wicked, or villainous individuals and that you should severely blame, damn, and punish them for their sins.

In RET the belief is that no people are bad, just people who at times act badly. People have the right to act badly because we are, after all, human and as such we are fallible.

The idea that life proves awful, terrible, horrible, or catastrophic when things do not go the way you would like them to go.

RET holds that nothing is so bad you can't take or stand it, even death. Taking an inconvenience and turning it into a catastrophe is a certain way of creating excessive anxiety and unneeded suffering.

The idea that emotional misery comes from external pressures and that you have little ability to control your feelings or rid yourself of depression and hostility.

At the core of RET theory is the belief that emotions largely come from our evaluations regarding events and not from the events themselves.

The idea that if something seems dangerous or fearsome, you must be terribly occupied with and upset about it.

In RET the belief is that worrying about an event is a waste of time in that worrying will not keep the feared event from occurring. A more beneficial procedure is to acknowledge that the feared event may transpire and that would be unfortunate but certainly not a tragedy.

The idea that you will find it easier to avoid facing many of life's difficulties and self-responsibilities than to undertake some rewarding forms of self-discipline.

RET postulates that facing a difficult situation squarely is often times the best way to deal with the situation and put it behind you if possible.

12   Rational Counseling With School Aged Populations

The idea that your past remains all important and that, because something once strongly influenced your life, it has to keep determining your feelings and behavior today.

In RET the belief is that the past has an influence over the present but does not determine the present. As humans, we have the ability to make significant behavioral change.

The idea that people and things should turn out better than they do; and that you have to view it as awful and horrible if you do not quickly find good solutions to life's hassles.

Evidence is lacking that anything should be different than it actually is and believing otherwise leads to blaming and anger. In RET the belief is that some situations are without perfect solutions but that this fact is not a terrible thing, just a reality.

The idea that you can achieve happiness by inertia and inaction or by passively and uncommittedly "enjoying yourself."

A good procedure is to be absorbed creatively in some activity that you enjoy. People who try to obtain happiness by passively interacting with life rarely lead rewarding lives.

The idea that you must have a high degree of order or certainty to feel comfortable; or that you need some supernatural power on which to rely.

So far as has been determined very few, if any, certainties exist in the universe.

Ch 3 Theory of Rational-Emotive Therapy 13

The idea that you can give yourself a global rating as a human and that your general worth and self-acceptance depend upon the goodness of your performance and degree that people approve of you.

In RET the belief is that your external accomplishments and your inherent value are two very different things. Combining the two usually leads to insecurity and disturbed emotional output in general (Ellis, 1977).

What is important to realize is that these twelve beliefs can take many, many forms. Each individual can have a slightly altered belief with variations on the wording. However, these twelve beliefs are at the core of emotional disturbance.

You may be wondering as to the significance of difference between the words annoyance and anger. Isn't this just semantics? RET theory always has distinguished between appropriate negative emotions such as annoyance and irritation and inappropriate negative emotions such as rage and anger. This IS an important distinction because it is believed that appropriate negative emotions will motivate an individual to change the circumstances involved whereas inappropriate negative emotions will usually lead to self-defeating behaviors which only make life more difficult. For example, if a student can remain only irritated at his/her inability to pass algebra, he/she will be in a better position than if he/she severely berates himself/herself thereby feeling angry and worthless.

PHILOSOPHY OF
RATIONAL-EMOTIVE THERAPY

RET is not only a type of psychotherapy but is also a philosophical approach to life and the world in which we live. The two go hand-in-hand.

The two major values of RET are survival and enjoyment. Walen, DiGuiseppe, and Wessler (1980) stated that anything that promotes your survival and happiness can be defined

14   Rational Counseling With School Aged Populations

as rational. Therefore, RET, not surprisingly, is hedonistic or pleasure seeking in its general philosophical stance. RET holds, however, that long term hedonism as opposed to short term hedonism is to be sought. An individual who lives for today may be sacrificing the future of the only life that we are certain to have. To live for today is desirable, but not at the expense of tomorrow.

RET theory holds that the methods of science are the best methods available for learning about ourselves, others, and our world (Walen, DiGuiseppe, & Wessler, 1980). Throughout therapy, clients are taught to think like scientists and search for proof of their beliefs. For example, to try different responses to situations is not uncommon. An adolescent I was working with had a problem relating to her step-mother. They continually seemed to fight which caused tension in the family. We brainstormed three potential responses when an argument seemed imminent:

1. simply leave the situation,

2. try as hard as possible to agree with the step-mother to appease her in hopes of avoiding an argument while holding onto your own opinion, or

3. verbally defend your position without becoming hurtful or "damning."

The next step was to gather data regarding whether the fight actually took place, how my client felt regarding what had happened, and how quickly things got back to normal.

After a few weeks of gathering data, clearly the best choice was to simply leave the situation as quickly as possible. This resulted in fewer arguments and fewer feelings of anxiety for my client. This may seem to be a way of actually avoiding the problem but what is important is that in this case apparently the step-mother was the one who was demanding and absolute. She, however, was not my client.

As might be imagined, assumptions, hunches, "gut feelings," and intuition are not valued as recommended ways of gathering ⟶

information. With intuition no "proof" is possible; therefore, no basis of fact is available on which to base that intuitive belief.

An 18-year-old male who was socially anxious could not work up the courage to ask out a certain member of the opposite sex for a date to the prom. He continually told himself, *"She'd never go out with me,"* to which I replied *"How can you be so sure? What proof do you have?"* He finally did ask her out and I wish I could tell you she accepted. She had already been asked and had accepted but told my client that had he asked earlier she would have attended with him. The evidence was now in and did not confirm the belief he had been carrying.

RET theory disputes traditional Freudian conclusions regarding the nature of emotional disturbance. Ellis (1962) has continually stated that individuals behave in given ways due to their conscious and preconscious thinking, beliefs, and attitudes about things and not because of early experiences. In RET the belief that individuals, even children, have many more options than they realize or choose to evaluate. What is important is what the student is thinking right here, right now. If a child is afraid of being left alone, the cause is not because the child was left alone and lacks security, but rather that the child believes being left alone, is terrible, awful, and a catastrophe and keeps reindoctrinating self with this belief almost daily.

Additionally, RET respectfully disagrees with strict behavioral theory and does not view man as a slave to the environment. While RET theory agrees that the environment is influential, man still chooses own emotional responses. If behavioral techniques do work in the elimination of anxiety, they work because by performing certain feared behaviors, clients realize nothing terrible is going to happen to them and therefore their self-talk changes. Instead of believing *"It is terrible to speak in front of people . . . I can't stand it"* they start to believe *"this isn't that bad . . . I can easily take this."* Why not directly attack the irrational self-talk that is causing the anxiety to begin with?

16   Rational Counseling With School Aged Populations

Finally, RET disagrees with the basic premise of client centered therapy in that unconditional love and acceptance are not necessary for change to occur. In fact, the idea or belief held by some clients that *"because my counselor loves and accepts me I must be lovable"* is quite frankly irrational. A therapist's beliefs about a client does not prove anything about the client's basic value as a human being. In all likelihood, these thoughts are at the core of the client's neurosis. Ellis tells a story of a client saying, *"Dr. Ellis, sometimes I don't think you like me"* to which he replied, *"You're right I don't. When that stops bothering you, you'll be ready to leave here."* This may seem harsh but the point is vital . . . it's **what YOU think that is important, not what others think.**

A topic that is widely discussed in our culture and is getting a great deal of media attention is the whole concept of self-esteem. While I know of no school of therapy in our culture that directly supports the following: the widely held belief is that individuals can be given a global rating according to their skills, accomplishments, and achievements. Many of the so-called "self-esteem" programs in American schools teach children that they are worthwhile BECAUSE they have certain attributes. To be worthwhile you have to have white teeth, the right clothes, and not perspire! The problem with this belief is that if you reverse the logic and say "without these highly valued attributes you are worthless" you are laying the groundwork for insecurity in literally thousands of children. This basic belief *("I am valuable because I can achieve or dance or . . . ")* is at the core of a tremendous amount of disturbance. A child with this belief will feel as though he/she has to earn his/her worth which can not be done indefinitely.

Is RET stating that people should not try to experience enjoyable situations that may involve earning recognition for a job well done? Not at all. RET holds that an unwise procedure is for individuals to esteem themselves because they believe their successes somehow make them more valuable or worthwhile. A better procedure is to be happy they were lucky enough to experience the success but don't overgeneralize the experience by making a reflection on to their inherent value. When a child obtains a good grade on his/her report

Ch 3   Theory of Rational-Emotive Therapy   17

card, harm could come from the child believing *"I am valuable because I did well."* This thinking will lead to insecurity due to the child's continued need to prove his/her worthwhileness. Besides, getting a good grade only means the child probably has a good grasp of that particular subject matter. Again, it has nothing to do with his/her inherent value.

In RET the belief is that the best way of avoiding unnecessary pain and suffering in life is through a basic philosophical change. If you can help children change irrational beliefs from absolute demands to preferences, from catastrophes to inconveniences, and from self-rating to self-accepting, they are in a much better position to enjoy life.

CHAPTER **4**

WHY USE RATIONAL-EMOTIVE THERAPY?

My first exposure to RET did not impress me. In undergraduate courses I had been in classes that focused on the major schools of psychotherapy and taught the distinctions between these schools. In graduate school I had the opportunity to actually do extensive reading on RET for a presentation.

After my research I was able to explain the basic underlying idea behind RET, that people cause a majority of their own difficulties by their own irrational thinking. My classmates asked questions that I now find to be very common when I try to explain the concepts of RET to individuals who are unfamiliar with these concepts. After my presentation, one of my classmates spoke up and said, *"You mean if someone steals my car I'm supposed to be happy about it?"* Another said, *"So is this guy Ellis just saying you should try to look on the bright side of life?"*

Experienced RET therapists will recognize these criticisms as two of the more popular misunderstandings regarding RET. The important point is that both stem from ideas about the workings of RET that are erroneous. Additionally, critics have contended that RET encourages clients to become excessively philosophical (if there is such a thing) and that they feel and sense experiences with less intensity. These concepts seem to express that those of us in the RET school have as our goal to turn children into repressive, unfeeling people. Nothing could be further from the truth.

As stated earlier, RET has always distinguished between appropriate feelings of sadness, concern, and irritation and inappropriate feelings of depression, preoccupation, and rage. If someone stole your car, of course you wouldn't be happy. However, a big difference exists between experiencing a rage attack and being upset that you are inconvenienced like this. No matter what you might think, having your car stolen is not a catastrophe, just an inconvenience.

My internship supervisor, Dr. George Harper, had to demonstrate RET for me to appreciate the beauty of the system. Even after watching Dr. Harper, I was skeptical until more and more of his clients kept looking healthier and healthier. I saw the light!

One of the major advantages of RET, especially if you work in a school, is that RET is very straight forward and direct. In a school setting, always a supply of children need assistance and a limited amount of services are available from counselors and psychologists. With RET, once the door is closed, typically only a short time is needed before you can begin to focus on treatment. It is not necessary to spend weeks delving through adolescents' earliest recollections and their dreams. The focus is on right here, right now. If a teenager is depressed, rest assured that he/she is doing something to depress self.

Hilbert, a 16-year-old Black male, came to see me because he was depressed. When he walked in the door, clearly I could observe he was troubled. His whole body sort of sagged and he walked as if he was in pain.

Within approximately 15 minutes, we had narrowed in on the problem. This boy was depressed because he kept telling himself and thinking to himself he was a worthless piece of garbage. He suffered from a long history of drug

20   *Rational Counseling With School Aged Populations*

and alcohol problems, and basically, he could not get or keep himself straight. Whenever he would fall off the abstinence wagon, he would tell himself, *"I'm no damn good . . . I'm just a druggie."*

With the use of RET principles, I tried to get this client to focus on his self-talk. My hope was to convince him that his drug problem did not prove anything about his value as a human. He wasn't a worthless person. He was a person with a drug problem. In order for him to focus his attention on his recovery he had to try to stop beating himself up. His continual self-downing was, in all likelihood, only increasing the chance of his slipping again. When he clearly understood that he was not a bad person but simply a person that at times acted badly you could literally see the cloud lift. Hilbert could now redirect this energy to fighting his addiction which would give him a better chance of succeeding.

Since RET tends to be directive and problem focused, it tends to be briefer than many other types of therapies. With RET, no valuable time is wasted waiting for the client to stumble upon the answer. If the therapist believes he/she has an insight into the problem, the interpretation is offered immediately. Many times clients are showing distinct signs of improvement only after a few sessions.

Even though RET is a problem centered approach it is also the type of treatment that can affect clients in broader ways. RET is nothing if it is not a philosophical way to view life and the world in which we live. As such it does not attempt just to stop anxiety attacks but does encourage also individuals to live life to the fullest. Frequently growth will be noticed in an area that was not even focused upon in therapy. Individuals can learn to take the philosophy of RET and apply it to other areas in their life. It brings to mind the parable, *"if you give a man a fish, he eats today. If you teach him to fish, he eats tomorrow."* In RET we believe *"if you help someone to feel better, they can make it through the day. If you help someone to think better, they will make it through tomorrow."* Or as my friend Dr. Harper told me, *"I used to think it was enough to make kids feel better but almost any adult can do that. I now know it is more important to teach them to think better."*

RET EMPOWERS PEOPLE!! It "arms" them with the knowledge and skills to help them deal with the day to day hassles. After that, they need not be dependent on you or any one else to help them in their lives. Some other therapies set up dependent relationships where the client needs to feel "loved" by the therapist. Such relationships only reinforce neurotic thinking that they need someone's approval and support to feel comfortable with themselves.

With nearly every child I ask them, *"how would you like it if no one ever could upset you again?"* They usually agree that they would like to have such skills. I tell my clients, *"There's not one person in a hundred that truly understands what I'm going to try and teach you. Not Ronald Reagan, George Bush, or the Pope have mastered these skills. Together we can discover a source of strength that very few will ever know."* As in any type of education, having a motivated client/ student never hurts.

WHEN DOESN'T RET WORK?

As in any theory of counseling, RET can not be all things to everyone. Some clients are difficult to reach for a number of reasons.

Mentally impaired youngsters often lack the ability to understand the concepts involved in RET. However, these children can be helped by focusing on teaching them rational coping statements rather than being concerned with disputing their irrational beliefs. They can learn these skills and benefit from them.

Some individuals will not accept the core premise of RET which is that we cause a majority of our own emotional misery and we are largely able to minimize our emotional suffering. Quite possibly some of these individuals do accept this idea but are unwilling to admit it because doing so would take away any reasons for their continual difficulties. Belief in RET places responsibility squarely on the shoulders of the client. Some people would sooner be dipped in hot oil than accept responsibilities for their actions. After all the best

22   *Rational Counseling With School Aged Populations*

philosophical arguments, you will still have a small percentage of clients who believe. *"No matter what you say my mom still makes me mad."* What is important to realize is that if clients are not willing to accept responsibility for their behavior, other schools of therapy will probably be unsuccessful as well.

Some critics of RET believe that RET can not be used with younger children. This is not true. Later in this book several examples will be given of techniques I use with younger children. What is true, of course, is that you must adjust the approach to fit the developmental level of the child. For example, rather than using a word like rational I might use the word "true" instead.

Other critics have stated that RET can only be helpful in the treatment of neurotics and can not be used with psychotics, obsessive compulsive disorders, and other disabilities. Ellis (1985) has illustrated the successful use of RET with psychotics. Ellis encouraged individuals not to berate themselves for their condition. Many times a client will produce what has been called **symptom stress.** For example, an individual who has a hard time with anger control who is becoming depressed due to his/her inability to control the anger. In Ellis' work with psychotics, he would teach these clients to accept themselves with their psychotic tendencies and never put themselves down for having them.

24   Rational Counseling With School Aged Populations

CHAPTER **5**

THE PRACTICE
OF RET

If you are experienced with school aged populations, then it will come as no surprise to you when I tell you, Counseling Children Can Be Very Different From Counseling Adults. This may seem like an obvious statement but I am surprised at the amount of times I hear a counselor describing the treatment plan with a child. The plan is not only inappropriate on developmental grounds alone, but also it smacks of middle class, mid-life values.

INITIAL CONSIDERATIONS

Adolescents hold concepts which often are different from adults. No general statements can be made that apply to all adolescents; however, commonly held concepts and behavior patterns are worthy of being considered.

1. Students tend to be extremely egocentric and believe that the world IS as they believe it to be. They have not had sufficient life experience to be able to understand or appreciate perspectives that are different from their own.

2. They tend to be insecure regarding their own skills and abilities but try desperately to hide these insecurities. Males tend to hide behind a mask of macho bravado while the females attempt to go happily along and refuse to acknowledge any difficulties whatsoever.

3. They are overly sensitive and have their feelings hurt easily due to their inner focus. The slightest look or wrong word can have a major effect on their self-confidence.

4. Since they do not have a clear sense of who they are, they tend to define themselves through their group associations. Additionally, they define themselves according to how others define them.

5. Students tend to experience wide mood swings and will go from elation to depression in a matter of minutes and then back to elation again. To predict when or how this will happen is difficult.

6. They constantly worry about being too much like everyone else so they strive for their own look and ideas. Conversely, they hate to be singled out or to be too different.

7. They are embarrassed by their parents but yet depend on them heavily. A large percentage have social anxiety and find it easier to withdraw from social contact even though by doing so they may be sacrificing some enjoyable activities.

8. Adolescents tend to overidealize and spend a lot of time and energy thinking about "what should be" rather than "what is." As such they have unrealistic expectations of themselves and others.

As you can see, adolescents tend to be paradoxical by their very nature. No wonder growing up is such a confusing time.

REFERRED AND SELF-REFERRAL

One of the most important differences between school-aged clients and adults is that a majority of referrals for children and adolescents are not self-referrals. This is not to say that students do not reach a point of sufficient emotional pain and seek out professional assistance through guidance counselors and school psychologists. However, a majority of referrals come from either teachers, parents, or other students.

The "other referred" client must be approached differently than self-referrals. Most students who get referred to a counselor do not realize or at least do not admit to having any type of problem. These clients can be resistant, suspicious, and even somewhat hostile. Typically, they have misconceptions about the therapy process.

I can recall a third-grade student who came to me as a result of a referral for frequent fighting.

Therapist: *Bobby, do you know why you are here today?*

Client: *No.*

T: *It's because some people think things could go better here at school.*

C: (No response)

T: *Do you know what a psychologist does?*

C: *They work with insane people.*

T: *Well, that's not exactly right. We work with lots different people who want to have things go better in their lives. I work with some of your classmates.*

C: *Like who? Is it Mark?*

Ch 5   The Practice of RET   27

T: *Well, that's not really important. How about if we talk about what happened at recess. I heard from other people but since you were there, I wanted to hear what really happened.*

RAPPORT

Establishing a positive working relationship is very important if therapy is to be effective. That is not to say that the relationship *is* the therapy as is so often the case in client centered therapy.

For an adolescent to express honestly how he/she feels, a reasonable amount of trust has to be present. To help establish this trusting relationship, Young's (1977) recommendations can be paraphrased as follows:

1. Allow long periods of uninterrupted listening. Many times adolescents have not had a chance to tell their side of the story so letting them talk freely without interruption can help build a strong therapeutic relationship.

2. Accept the client's reality perspective regardless of how distorted or limited it may be. Such acceptance will make the therapist an ally rather than an opponent.

3. Discuss openly your own opinions and attitudes. By being open and direct with the client, it will encourage the same type of openness. Also, most adults are somewhat unapproachable for teenagers. They are curious what this adult life is really like.

4. Allow a companion to sit in on a session. A companion can be useful to help relax the client. Young also wrote about using the companion to make a point.

5. Give the adolescent priority. If a client is brought in by parents, see the teenager first. This can give the young person evidence that you value his/her time and want to receive his/her input. Try telling

28   *Rational Counseling With School Aged Populations*

your secretary "No calls while I'm with Jim" as a little technique to show you really do value what the client has to say.

6. Extract from parents an initial concession. It doesn't have to be a major concession but a small increase in allowance or curfew can be beneficial. This can give the teenager the idea that the therapist has some power over the parents. It will, at the very least, make the client more open to the new relationship.

I would like to add a few simple techniques for working with smaller children.

1. Try not to stare continuously at the child. This usually creates a sense of anxiety that is detrimental to the goals of therapy. You can observe the child in short segments and this will allow the client to examine you and the room.

2. Try not to adopt a little person's voice. Children can tell that something is forced about this interaction. Kids are sort of like sharks: they can sense staged gimmicks like blood in the water. By the same token, a totally appropriate and recommended procedure is for you to become more childlike. I would never "high five" with my banker but I've never met a grade schooler who didn't love to "high five." If you feel comfortable doing things like that, give it a try.

3. Try getting on the child's level. If you are at a table and chair try putting your hands flat on the table and your head on your hands. Children seem to open up when adults adopt a more passive posture. Sitting on the floor as opposed to being in a chair also can be very effective to take the formalness out of a situation.

4. Try not to "grill" the child. Too many questions can be overwhelming to a child. I'll never forget a little six-year-old girl asking me, *"Why are you asking me all this stuff?"* The point was well taken. Get a basic

Ch 5   The Practice of RET   29

background of information from others if that is at all possible.

Walen et al. (1980) made the suggestion that the need is not to focus on THE problem; instead focus on nearly any problem a client presents as the starting point of therapy. Exceptions to this rule do exist such as when a child is engaging in behavior that could be injurious to self or others.

A note of caution might be made in that many children (and adults for that matter) will present a problem that is not within their control. For example, a child may say, *"I'd like you to help me to get my dad to stop drinking."* A teenager may say, *"I'm depressed because my girlfriend broke up with me."* Often possibly the focus of the presenting problem can be changed. Following is an example of such a technique.

Therapist: *Mike, I understand that you're sad and that your girlfriend broke up with you. I'm afraid there is nothing we can do about her choice. Maybe it would be best to focus on what we can control.*

Client: *You mean I have to just accept that she's taking Larry to the prom instead of me?*

T: *You don't have to accept anything. You can always make yourself miserable worrying and demanding that she come back to you. The problem with that is you are pretending you have power that you just don't have. Life just isn't like that. We can't get what we want just by demanding it.*

ASSESSMENT

When working with younger populations try to accurately assess their basic thinking skills. One of the first fundamental questions to address is, *"Is this child a concrete or abstract thinker?"* An unwise assumption would be that because a student is 14 years old, he/she is an abstract thinker. My

30   *Rational Counseling With School Aged Populations*

experience has been that some are not. In fact, most likely when compared with all other 14 year olds, your clients will have poorer abstracting skills. This may be a big part of the reason they are your client!

Some counselors feel that formal assessment is not necessary and that they can assess a child's thinking skills during the initial stages of therapy. For many of your clients this may be true. With all clients a continuous stream of behavioral data is pouring out. Many therapists miss important data believing that assessment is only done in a formalized procedure with paper and pencil tests. I've learned a great deal about children while observing them in their classroom, at recess, in the hall, or even in the community at large. One advantage school counselors have over private therapists is that school counselors usually have some experience with a child before they start therapy. This can be helpful as opposed to starting from scratch. However, it can also lead to preconceived ideas about the child that are inaccurate.

I don't have a hard and fast rule for trying to decide whether I'm going to use a formalized assessment battery. I usually start with informal techniques and hope to get adequate information in that manner. If after I have tried this approach, I still feel the need for more data, I will use some formalized assessment techniques.

With informal assessment try to obtain an understanding of the kinds of issues formalized assessment procedures may overlook such as:

> Does the child use absolute-type language (shoulds, musts, ought to)?

> What is the basic troubling emotion?

> What is the child doing to cause that emotion?

> What type of disputation will be effective with the child?

> Does the child view the situation as problematic?

Can they judge the consequences of an act?

How well can they tolerate frustration?

What interests do they have?

What would they be willing to work towards?

An excellent source of information for some of these questions is the child's classroom teacher. One had best be careful not to assume that the child's teacher is a totally unbiased source of information. Teachers are people too and as such are prone to the same type of dogmatic, unyielding thinking that is at the core of most emotional disturbance.

In some cases a new question arises, namely, *"Is this a teacher problem or a student problem?"* Teachers may have unrealistic expectations or a personality conflict may exist with a student. Let's face it, some students are easier to be around than others.

The recommendation is that if you determine the difficulty to be a teacher problem, you actively intervene with the teacher if that is possible. Hopefully, the teacher is approachable and is willing to adjust his/her beliefs regarding the child. I have heard several stories of colleagues who think, *"Well, I'll give in to Mr. Johnson and play along on this one even though I don't think Billy is the problem."* The difficulty with this approach has nothing to do with ethics or the wasted time and energy. The real problem is that three weeks later another little "Billy" will pop up and dear old Mr. Johnson will place that child at your door. Later in this book, an entire chapter will be devoted to working with teachers that contains recommendations for dealing with such situations.

At times the teacher is not going to give one inch in demands on the student and all your interventions will be ineffective. After all, teachers have the right to be wrong just like the rest of us. At this point, a procedure that may be helpful is to teach the student to cope with the teacher the best way possible. Students might as well know now that not everyone will treat them fairly in life, no matter how much they dislike it.

32   Rational Counseling With School Aged Populations

Several different procedures may be utilized to proceed with a standardized assessment. To gather information from the parents is important, but one must be careful to not be unnecessarily influenced by the parents' perceptions. Remember, the parents' goals for the child may not be the child's goals. In fact, the parents' agendas also may be completely unrealistic.

Tape and Worksheet

With my high school and junior high aged clients I have used a technique which has been beneficial as an assessment tool as well as a therapeutic tool. At the end of our first session, I usually give to my client an audio cassette tape and a worksheet. The tape contains a pre-recorded message of basic RET material that is important for them to know. I tell them to listen to the tape as many times as they have to in order to answer the questions on the worksheet. This procedure not only teaches RET concepts but also allows me to assess a client's motivation and willingness to work in therapy. Informally, I find a high, positive correlation between homework completion and progress in therapy.

As school counselors will tell you, always more students are waiting to receive some type of counseling than can be seen. The use of the tape and the worksheet helps me to make important decisions regarding which students are ready to take an active role in their treatment. This is not to say I am encouraging that difficult and resistant clients not receive treatment. With therapy, an optimal time exists during which you have a better chance of being successful. To work with students when they are ready to work is beneficial.

I recall a 16-year-old male I saw one morning. George had been diagnosed as suffering from depression. A local psychiatrist had prescribed anti-depressant medication which was causing all too familiar side effects of dryness of the mouth and eyes as well as overall difficulty getting started in the morning. After giving him the tape and worksheet at 10:30 a.m., he had the worksheet completed and back to me by 1:00 p.m. that afternoon. He had completed the tape over his lunch hour. Obviously, he was a motivated client and we began to work immediately. He made excellent progress. No matter what homework assignment I gave him, George completed it on time.

I would be happy to make a copy of the work sheet and cassette tape if any of the readers would like to have one. Just send a blank cassette and a SASE to the following address:

Jerry Wilde
East Troy Elementary School
P.O. Box 257
East Troy, WI 53120

Feeling Thermometer

One assessment technique that I use quite often is called the feeling thermometer. A student is asked to rate the intensity of a feeling from one to 100 with one being the lowest and 100 being the most intense. As mentioned earlier, children often times lack the verbal sophistication necessary to communicate the range of emotions they experience. The feeling thermometer allows the child another means of conveying how he/she feels.

Rational Sentence Completion Task

Appearing for the first time in any published form is the *Rational Sentence Completion Task* (RSCT). The scale is composed of several partially completed sentences (see Figure 1 in the Appendix). The client is asked to complete the sentence in whatever manner he/she feels is appropriate. The major advantage of the RSCT is that it is not a forced choice for the client. In the above-mentioned scales the list of possible responses is forced upon the client and can be limiting.

Play Therapy

Play therapy techniques such as the use of puppets can allow a child to express uncomfortable emotions. This game can give you access to a child's internal dialogue that otherwise might not be accessible. Have the child perform a puppet show of a conflict and listen for clues to his/her irrational thinking.

Checklists

Several checklists are designed to be used with students. These checklists are attempts to directly assess students' thinking in terms of rationality. *Children's Survey of Rational Beliefs* (Knaus, 1974) is composed of Form B (ages 7 through 10) and Form C (ages 10 through 13). Each form is a multiple choice instrument that presents typical developmental scenarios such as peer and school related situations. For copy of Form B see Figure 2 in the Appendix. For copy of Form C see Figure 3 in the Appendix. For answer keys to both forms see Figure 4 in the Appendix.

The Idea Inventory (Kassinove, Crisci, & Tiegerman, 1977) measures eleven irrational ideas which are each assessed by three statements. A student reads a statement and has to respond either (1) agree, (2) uncertain or (3) disagree. For a copy of the *Idea Inventory,* see Figure 5 in the Appendix.

One drawback of these scales is that they lack normative, reliability, or validity data (Bernard & Joyce, 1984.) However, these scales can be used to assist in assessment and it could be argued that their face validity is high. If a student circles "agree" to the statement *"I can't help but feel depressed when others let me down"* that tells you something important about that student's thinking.

Some individuals have criticized the use of such scales stating that they only measure the extent to which individuals have learned the language of RET. Another way to view this situation is to realize that learning the basic concepts and language is a necessity for adolescents and children to benefit from RET. These scales can measure individuals progress in this important area. I've yet to see a child improve using RET who did not have a clear understanding of the importance of using rational language. I tell my clients, *"how we talk out of our mouths is a lot like the way we talk to ourselves. If I hear you saying things like 'he shouldn't' and 'it's terrible' I've got a pretty good idea that you think things like that but don't say them. That's what we've got to change if you're going to feel better."* People will never learn to walk the walk if they can't talk the talk!

THE ABC'S OF RET

Ellis (1962) devised a system to aid in problem assessment and identification which can be used in a variety of ways and has been expanded upon by other RET therapists. The system is known as the ABC's of RET. Also a "D" and "E" will be discussed later but for right now lets just focus on the A, B, and C.

In this system the "A" stands for the activating event (what happened), "B" stands for the belief (what you thought), and "C" stands for the consequence (what you felt.)

A—activating event (what happened)

B—belief (what you thought)

C—consequence (what you felt)

Ellis (1985) stated that the major advantage of the ABC's comes from the simplicity of the system. This makes using the ABC's especially beneficial for working with children and adolescents.

As stated earlier, the ABC's may be used in many ways. Some therapists start with the "C" (consequence or feeling) because it's typically the first thing the client offers to you.

Therapist: *How are you today, Bill?*

Client: *Not very good today.*

T: *Can you tell me more about that?*

C: *I'm depressed.* (Consequence)

36   Rational Counseling With School Aged Populations

Notice the child in this example is able to clearly and easily identify his feelings. Most of you know this is not always the case.

Quite commonly the client will give initially the "A" or what happened and you then go in search of the "C" or emotional response.

> T: *So what would you like to talk about?*
>
> C: *My mom and dad are getting a divorce.* (Note: This is the event or "A").
>
> T: *And Alice, you feel how about that.*
>
> C: *Pretty bad . . . like maybe it's my fault.* (Author's note: This feeling of guilt is the "C").

Many times children lack emotional vocabulary. They know that they're upset but lack the linguistic skill and experience to identify and accurately label their feelings.

> Therapist: *Can you tell me how you're feeling today?*
>
> Mary: *O.K. I guess.*
>
> T: *Just O.K.?*
>
> M: *Well, I'm confused about how I feel. I feel all mixed up inside.*
>
> T: *Well, see if you can make me understand.*
>
> M: *Well, I hate Mr. Wilson, my math teacher.*
>
> T: *Why's that?*
>
> M: *He gave me a detention because he said I talked back to him. I have to bring my mom and dad to meet with him and the principal.*

(Author's note: At this point, we have indications of anxiety over the upcoming meeting and anger at her teacher. I'd also like to check to see if there is some "self-downing" that usually accompanies these two.)

T: *You sound pretty scared.*

M: *Yeah, my folks will kill me.* (Author's note: Notice the awfulizing.)

T: *It also sounds like you feel like Mr. Wilson isn't being very fair and that you're pretty mad at him.*

M: *He's a shithead!* (Notice the damning of poor Mr. Wilson.)

T: *Mary, I'm also wondering if you're beating yourself up just a little because of this whole mess. Can you hear yourself saying things like "Am I ever stupid. I ought to know better."*

M: *Not exactly those words but close.*

T: *What do you hear then? What tapes are you playing in your head?*

M: *That I'm a no good piece of garbage.*

THE ULTIMATE GOAL OF RET IS TO HELP CLIENTS BECOME MORE AWARE OF THEIR IRRATIONAL SELF-TALK AND HELP THEM TO REPLACE THEIR OLD "TAPES" WITH NEW, RATIONAL ONES. THE ABC'S CAN SERVE THIS PURPOSE QUITE NICELY.

After you have the "C" clearly distinguished and agreed upon, then is time to go after the "A" or Activating event. Again, some clients are, by nature, very much able to define clearly and concisely "A." Many children are not. In their egocentricism, they believe every trivial thought and detail needs to be included. Unlike some client-centered therapies, which are non-directive and will let the client talk endlessly,

RET is directive and encourages the therapist to help the client focus on the important details.

In my very first RET session as a 22-year-old intern, I had a significant problem getting at the "A." Having had Counseling 101, I sat listening (actively!) as my client, a 17-year-old female who was self-referred, rambled on for nearly an hour about her prom date, parents, pets, and a host of other unrelated topics. At the end of the session, my internship supervisor asked me how things had gone. I told him I was frustrated in that the girl kept "switching the A." He told me you can be much more direct. Stop the client, interrupt if you have to, and say something like, *"How does this relate to your feeling depressed?"* Another suggestion is to say something like, *"Whoa, slow down, you're confusing me here. What's the part that lead up to your anger?"* Remember, with RET, no need exists to set up any type of transference relationship. Or as Dr. Harper so succinctly put it, *"That 'liking' stuff just gets in the way."* The goal here is to establish the A, not to lead the client to believe you are the most empathetic human who has ever lived and will listen without hesitation to every utterance he/she has to say.

In some instances "C" can become "A" as is the case with symptom stress. A client who was angry most of the time is now trying to control his/her anger. When they slip up and anger themselves, they become depressed over their inability to master this difficulty. The ABC might be something like the following:

   A. The client "blows his/her stack" in history.

   B. *"What an idiot I am for getting angry at such an insignificant thing."*

   C. Depression

After you clearly have the "A" and "C" understood and agreed upon, then is time to focus on the "B" (belief). As we shall see, the "B" is where the client is having the belief or thought that is upsetting.

Ch 5   The Practice of RET   39

Many times a vital procedure is to point out clearly to the client that A (getting dumped by your girlfriend) did not cause C (depression). Many people, including learned adults, firmly believe this notion that outside events cause feelings. To use examples with children is helpful in showing them that B causes C. Of all the examples I've heard, I prefer "the blind man on a bus."

Therapist: *John, I know you think that Sally breaking up with you is making you sad but it's really something else. It's what you're thinking or believing about it.*

Client: *I don't understand. What do you mean how I'm thinking about it?*

T: *Well, let me tell you a story to see if we can both be a little more on the same page with this. Let's pretend we're riding on a bus and all of a sudden you get poked in the ribs. How would you feel?*

C: *Probably at first scared.*

T: *OK, you'd be scared, why?*

C: *Because I'd be afraid I was going to get hurt.*

T: *So you'd say what to yourself.*

C: *I'd say something like "I might get hurt or killed."*

T: *OK, now you turn to see what poked you and you see it was a blind man who accidentally poked you. How would you feel now?*

C: *Relieved.*

T: *Right, because you'd be thinking what?*

C: *That I won't be hurt, he didn't mean to poke me.*

40   *Rational Counseling With School Aged Populations*

T: *Good, but now look at this. You've got the same A, getting poked, causing two different C's, scared and then relieved. How could that be?*

C: *I don't know.*

T: *Well, let me tell you. It couldn't be because A can't cause C. B causes C. Do you see that here you thought or believe you might be hurt and then you saw you weren't in danger and thought something completely different. That's why you felt differently.*

C: *Yeah, I see what you mean now.*

A more expanded version of this example will follow later in this book. What's important is that you now have a frame of reference to overlay your client's problem. I'll add here that I usually draw this process out on a piece of paper and let the client keep the paper to help himself/herself if he/she gets confused.

A. Poked in the ribs

B1. "I might get hurt!"

B2. "He didn't mean to poke me."

C1. Scared, afraid

C2. Relieved

To make certain a client truly understands this example have the student repeat it back to you or have him/her make up own story. Some clients will look you in the eye and nod as if they understand but when you check for comprehension they are quite confused but didn't want to say so.

The purpose in teaching the ABC's is to get clients to integrate this thinking into their everyday lives. With enough practice clients can leave the model totally behind. Eventually, this is desired because to sit down and perform a drawn out ABC each time you become upset is not very practical.

A few simple reminders relating to anger, depression, and anxiety are as follows:

Anger—Usually stems from some type of demanding.

Depression—Usually stems from self-downing or damning the world.

Anxiety—Usually stems from awfulizing or making an event worse than it actually is in reality.

Obviously, these are oversimplified but more times than not these are the core irrational beliefs associated with these emotions.

RATIONAL VERSUS IRRATIONAL

At this point, try making some increasingly subtle clarifications with the client between rational and irrational beliefs. In an earlier chapter of this book a list is provided of the most common irrational beliefs. What exactly about a belief makes it either rational or irrational?

When working with elementary school aged children, I like to use the terms "true" and "false" beliefs. Examples are usually helpful in the explanation, especially if the child is not at a level of cognitive functioning where he/she can use abstract thought easily.

Therapist: *Do you know the difference between true and false?*

Client: *Yeah, if something is true, then it really is that way. If its false, then it's not.*

42   *Rational Counseling With School Aged Populations*

T: *In this world we have two kinds of beliefs: true and false. The true ones we know to be true because we've got proof. With false beliefs we've got no proof. For example, if I told you, "I believe you don't like detention," would that be a true or a false beliefs?*

C: *True!*

T: *O.K., what proof do we have?*

C: *You asked me and I told you.*

T: *What else?*

C: *I don't know.*

T: *Well, people tend to do things they like and I've never seen you at detention without a teacher making you go. If I said "I believed you like basketball," true or false?*

C: *True.*

T: *What proof do we have?*

C: *I play it and watch it a lot.*

T: *You're also wearing a Phoenix Suns jersey. What if I said I believed the sun isn't coming up tomorrow?*

C: *That would be false. The sun comes up no matter what.*

T: *So I don't really have any proof do I? It's just a crazy idea. Let me ask you this, how would believing the sun isn't coming up help me or hurt me?*

Ch 5   The Practice of RET   43

C: *I don't think it would help you. It might hurt you because people would think you're crazy. Or you'd be really scared.*

T: *Right, true beliefs usually help us and false beliefs don't help us and sometimes hurt us.*

At this point, the transition is eased into the clients thinking regarding whatever problem situation they are presenting. Are they demanding the world be different than it is? Are they awfulizing? Or are they putting themselves down?

Many times clients want to know how they can be certain that they are thinking rational and not irrational thoughts. I tell them that the *"proof is in the pudding."* If they are feeling angry, depressed, or extremely uptight, they are probably thinking some irrational thoughts. If they are not bothered by excessively upsetting emotions, they're probably doing a fine job with their thinking.

Often clients, especially children, have a hard time spontaneously changing an irrational belief into a rational belief. To simply restate their irrational belief into a rational belief may be easy for you, but by doing so you are using your language which may not feel comfortable or natural to your client. A much better procedure is to have your client produce his/her own rational statement. How does one help a nine year old accomplish such a feat? Different therapist use different ways, but I have found the use of *Rational Emotive Imagery (REI)* to be very effective.

RATIONAL EMOTIVE IMAGERY (REI)

REI is a technique that has many applications. A detailed analysis of how to use REI to combat irrational beliefs will come later in this book. At this point we're concerned with producing a rational statement in the client's own words.

You start by having your client place his/her feet firmly on the floor and get comfortable in the chair. Next, explain that you are going to lead him/her through the event (A)

44   *Rational Counseling With School Aged Populations*

in the person's mind. You want the individual to imagine he/she is actually at the event.

> T: *Close your eyes now and take a deep breath. Let it out slowly and, as you do, realize that you are only aware of my voice. Listen very closely.*
>
> *Think back to when you got into that fight at recess. Imagine you're back on the playground. See all the children on the swings, hear the sound of voices, feel the sun on your body. When you truly can imagine that, wiggle your finger to let me know.*
>
> *Now, imagine Stephen taking your ball away. Remember how angry you got. Go ahead and feel that anger again. When you can feel it, wiggle your finger.*

(It is important to watch for behavioral signs of the emotion. With anger, look for movement along the side of the face as the jaw gets set. Also, nostrils flair. With depression look for downward curling of the mouth to a slight frown. With anxiety look for behavior such as fidgeting, excessive movement.)

> *Once you're there, stay there for awhile. Feel how angry you are.*

(Pause here for 30 - 60 seconds)

> *OK. Now I want you to calm yourself down. Stay there in your mind and calm yourself down. Keep working until you've calmed yourself all the way down. When you get there, wiggle your finger.* (Author's note: This may take 20 seconds or several minutes.)
>
> *Now, I want you to take a deep breath and when you breath out, open your eyes.*
>
> *Tell me what you said to yourself to calm yourself down.*

Ch 5   The Practice of RET   45

C: *I said, "I don't have to have that ball. There are plenty of others."*

Most clients can very easily perform this activity and usually can produce a rational statement, even on the first try.

This may sound too simple but it has worked with an overwhelming majority of clients. The fact that individuals can calm themselves gives support to Ellis' idea that we really do have more choices than we are aware.

DISPUTATION

A vitally important part of RET is the point at which the irrational beliefs at "B" are disputed or challenged. This is the "D" which is known as **disputation.**

Disputation can take many forms but the goals of each technique are the same: TO GET THE STUDENT TO EXAMINE HIS/HER BELIEFS AND PHILOSOPHIES ABOUT LIFE AND DETERMINE WHETHER OR NOT THEY MAKE SENSE. Are these beliefs helpful in obtaining your goals or are they making your life more difficult? If through the process of disputation a student reaches the conclusion that his/her beliefs are irrational, then they are helped to replace these old, destructive beliefs with new, rational beliefs. This is the point at which real work in therapy takes place.

As mentioned earlier, RET employs cognitive, emotive, and behavioral techniques. Usually, a combination of the above mentioned modes of disputation are used with a client. To be certain which techniques will be most effective with a given client is difficult and that is why using a number of techniques through the course of therapy is best.

Cognitive Disputations

Most cognitive techniques involve questions that are aimed at getting the client to question the logic of his/her beliefs (Walen et al., 1980.) Most schools of therapy other than RET

46   *Rational Counseling With School Aged Populations*

discourage "why" questions but at this juncture of treatment in RET, they can be very effective.

Client: *He can't call me a name and just get away with it!*

Therapist: *Henry, why can't he?*

C: *People would think I'm a wimp.*

T: *Why is it so important what those people think of you?*

C: *I just don't like it, that's all.*

T: *Why do things have to work out the way you want?*

C: *Well they don't have to but I want them to.*

T: *Think for a minute and tell me if that attitude is going to help you or hurt you?*

C: *What attitude?*

T: *The attitude that says I have to have things my way just because I want them that way?*

C: *I don't know . . . probably it won't help.*

T: *Why not?*

C: *Because nobody really gives a shit what I want anyway.*

T: *When it comes right down to it, not many people care enough to do anything about it and demanding that they do care is not going to change anything.*

Through cognitive disputation clients hopefully learn to reflexively think *"Do I have any evidence or proof for that* belief?" Eventually, this type of questioning can become second nature as clients start to take control of their thinking. Before this happens they will probably need a lot of help in breaking the old patterns and substituting new patterns. Clients find it easier to stay disturbed than to change and will fall back into old habits very easily.

Humor and Exaggeration. One technique of disputation that I use quite often is humor and exaggeration. Humor can be used very effectively with a client to illustrate the awfulizing. Since awfulizing is exaggerating an events "badness" the use of exaggeration to a ridiculous extent can be eye opening. You want to establish an atmosphere where a client can tell that you are not serious or he/she will feel belittled.

C: *But I can't get a "C" on a math test. I couldn't stand that.*

T: *You're right. That would be the worst thing I've ever heard. That would be a catastrophe! I can't even think about that because it is so entirely horrible.*

C: *Wow, do I really sound like that?*

T: *Not quite that bad but close. Can you see that if you stop demanding that you do well, and just prefer that you do well, you'll be more relaxed and probably do better?*

Ellis (1985) told a humorous story that is designed to get clients to stop worrying about things they can't control and focusing on things they can control.

T: *If the Martians ever visited Earth, they might laugh themselves half to death.*

C: *Why is that?*

T: *Because they would see us Earthlings desperately trying to change things like how our parents treated us which we can not possibly*

48   *Rational Counseling With School Aged Populations*

*change and refusing to change things we
certainly can change, like ourselves. They
wouldn't know what to think.*

Paradoxical Intention. Occasionally the use of paradoxical
intention can be beneficial. The idea with this disputation
technique is to tell the client to do the exact opposite of
what you really want the person to do. With an anxious
client you might say, *"I want you to try and worry only
15 minutes a day from 12:00 to 12:15."* This is a drastic
method and is not recommended except for use with highly
resistive clients who will not work on other forms of disputation.
As you may have guessed, this type of technique does not
attack the core underlying beliefs that are causing the child
to be disturbed in the first place.

Modeling of Disputation. The use of modeling of
disputations can be very effective as well. As mentioned earlier,
children are egocentric to the point that the idea that someone
else may have a similar problem can be completely foreign
to them. Sharing personal problems with clients can be very
powerful with children and adolescents.

Joan: *I'm so sick of dealing with this diabetes. The
needles, the diet, why can't I be normal like
everyone else?*

T: *It's tough isn't it? I know because I have some
of the same type of hassles. I used to think
giving myself injections was terrible and awful
but I realize now it's not, it's still only bad,
not 110% bad. I wish you and I didn't have
to do this but we don't have a choice.*

C: *But don't you want to just scream your head
off sometimes?*

T: *Not really because it won't do anything to change
the situation. We've both got two choices: (1)
accept our bad luck and concentrate on staying
as healthy as we can so we can enjoy ourselves
as much as possible or (2) spend virtually all*

Ch 5   The Practice of RET   49

our time pissing and moaning about our bad luck. I'll tell you what, if I thought complaining would make me feel better, I might complain all day long but we both know that's silly.

Deep Relaxation. Cognitive distraction is a technique Ellis (1985) discussed that can be effective with resistant clients. He cautioned readers that distraction is merely a temporary method and is not changing the clients philosophical belief system which is at the core of his/her disturbance. Teaching children to perform deep muscle relaxation or meditation may help them when they have upset themselves and most clients can learn such techniques. This can be especially useful with children and adolescents suffering from anxiety disorders. The states of deep relaxation and anxiety are not complimentary and can not exist simultaneously. If a child can learn to be aware of the early signs of anxiety and can quickly practice relaxation exercises it may be possible to dramatically reduce the intensity and duration of anxiety related episodes.

Behavioral Disputations

Behavioral disputations can take many forms. RET has encouraged individuals to actively face their fears as a way of overcoming them. For example, if a student is afraid of asking out a member of the opposite sex for a date, have him/her ask out five a week or as many as is needed to overcome this fear. The more an individual performs this feared activity, the more they will realize that nothing catastrophic actually is going to occur and the anxiety will fade away.

Reinforcement. Ellis (1985) described the use of reinforcement after the client has completed a homework assignment as another means of behavioral disputation. For school-aged children this can be accomplished through cooperation with the parents. An agreed upon reinforcer can be administered by a mother or father after a child has practiced his/her guided imagery. This is doubly beneficial because it gets mom and/or dad involved in the child's therapy.

Poll Taking. One of the most effective techniques of behavioral disputation is what I call "poll taking." This is a process by which a client takes a poll of other individuals to determine the accuracy of his/her perceptions. For example, seven-year-old Naomi was sent to me with the presenting problem of low self-esteem. She had been molested by her step-father and since that time had insisted that she was "the ugliest girl." Since high self-esteem can really be defined as a state in which you are not too concerned with others opinions of you. Conversely, low self-esteem may be thought of as being unnecessarily concerned with others opinion of you. Because Naomi was only seven, I realized that she would not be able to grasp the abstract concept that it's not important what other people think of you, what counts is what you think of yourself. I decided to try a rather inelegant approach.

I had the child take a clip board and piece of paper and write at the top, "Do you hate me?" The possible responses were simply "yes" or "no." We then preceded to take a poll of individuals we ran into in the hall and around the school. As you might have guessed, no one responded that they hated Naomi and we used those data often in further sessions.

Emotive Disputations

Rational Emotive Imagery. Emotive techniques such as Rational Emotive Imagery (REI), forceful self-dialogue, and shame attacking exercise are also commonly used as part of a disputation.

REI is a technique I use quite frequently not only to produce a client's own, individualized rational statement, but to also actually treat and combat existing irrational ideas. A client is taught to perform REI regarding the situation that is troubling them at least three times a day. Once they become proficient, they can do REI almost anywhere. For example, an adolescent with social anxiety is taught to imagine a typical anxiety provoking situation. Once he/she can clearly visualize such a situation, the adolescent is to use rational coping statements to change own feelings from inappropriate to more appropriate feelings.

If children can visualize decently and will consistently practice, you will see a reduction in anxiety. They are being exposed to a situation they had defined as "terrible" and "horrible" and have now been able to experience it (albeit only mentally) without any catastrophes occurring.

The same technique can work well with students who have a difficult time controlling their anger. Have the student revisualize a situation in which they angered self. After he/she has regained feelings of anger, tell the student to, *"Calm yourself down."* As a result of this technique, the child or adolescent can learn some valuable skills that may very well keep him/her out of difficulties in school.

Shame Attacking Exercise. Shame attacking exercise focus on encouraging a resistant client to perform a publicly "shameful" or embarrassing act (Ellis, 1985). As mentioned earlier, some clients will not actively work on their irrational thinking but will perform the exercise and undermine their own beliefs.

A 16-year-old girl with low self-esteem was perfectionistic especially with matters related to her appearance. Being unable to get Phyllis to examine her own crazy thinking (which focused on her dire need for love and attention), I challenged and prodded her into coming to school without make-up or her hair done. She finally was able to do such a thing and amazingly, actually lived through the day! After this, she was more willing to work on her self-talk, I think, because for the first time, she truly believed it wouldn't be horrible if others didn't approve of her. It had to be proven to her and apparently it was.

Forceful Dialogue. Forceful dialogue can be used in a number of creative ways. A client can on the one hand, verbalize his/her own irrational beliefs and turn around and confront them rationally. The same procedure can be accomplished with a tape recorder playing the irrational voice and the client speaking the rational voice.

Irrational: *What an idiot I am for the way I acted in math class.*

52   *Rational Counseling With School Aged Populations*

Rational: *I'm not an idiot, I'm a person who sometimes acts idiotically. I just proved that I'm fully human.*

I: *No one will want to be with me.*

R: *It is highly unlikely that no one will want to be with me. Even if they did reject me, it wouldn't kill me.*

I: *Life sure sucks!*

R: *Life does have some bad stuff occasionally, but where is it written in stone that life has to be easy and simple?*

Destroying Power-figure of Therapist. A final technique that is worth mentioning is as much a matter of trust building as disputation. I often find that my clients view me as an authority figure who has power over them. This may be counter-productive to therapy. By demonstrating that you are not a member of the "controlling forces" you can encourage trust. Many times trust allows clients to work harder at disputing their irrational ideas.

This can be accomplished in a number of ways. I might use a word like "shit" or "damn" which is something a principal or teacher would never do. I only do this on rare occasions with, for example, a juvenile delinquent who would definitely have such a word in his/her vocabulary.

If you can spend some time talking about current sporting events or the latest cassette by a popular musical group it can really breakdown the walls between you and lower the suspicion of the client. I have a sticker of the musical group "Anthrax" displayed prominently in my brief case that is not there by accident. I've had literally dozens of student's say to me, *"You're the dude that likes Anthrax."*

Don't try this technique if it would be forced and seem artificial. Therapists who try this and come off appearing ungenuine and phony do nothing to encourage sharing and trust.

54   Rational Counseling With School Aged Populations

CHAPTER **6**

DEPRESSION

One of the most commonly reported problems when a child is referred is depression. Nothing gets a parent's or teacher's attention quicker than self-injurious talk or behavior. However, my experience has been that many, if not most, childhood depressives do not present depressive behavior. They may be more likely to be acting out their difficulties and the depression can be easily missed.

CASE EXAMPLE

Thomas, an eight-year-old caucasian, was referred because of somewhat violent and dangerous playtime activity. Within the past month, he had choked a classmate, hit a crossing guard with a rock and told the librarian to *"go f _ _ _ yourself."* What was presented as a child with poor anger and impulse control, as well as lacking social skills, soon became more complicated. Upon the initial session, Thomas could fairly well articulate that, to put it in his words, *"I hate my guts."* In general, he was depressed and specifically did not see how anyone could value him, especially since he thought he was worthless and unlovable.

Many younger children simply lack the verbal skills to explain how they feel and can only name a few feeling words such as angry and happy. Every feeling has to somehow fit within these two categories. Naturally what follows is that

Ch 6   Depression   55

feelings such as hurt, shame, and guilt, get described as mad or angry by the child.

Obviously, Thomas also suffered from low self-esteem. Please note that I will not use the terms depression and low self-esteem interchangeably. True, these difficulties are related; however, also true is that many individuals with low self-esteem do not progress (or regress) to depression.

BERATING SELF

Bernard and Joyce (1984) pointed out that the normal human emotion is to feel bad when we perform poorly. Most people, however, do not put themselves down to an extent where they feel excessively sad and worthless for an extended period of time. In fact, many individuals are motivated by the uncomfortable feelings they experience when they perform less than perfectly. Some clients berate themselves so severely when they fail or are rejected that depression results.

Hopefully, by now you are realizing that RET maintains that an event (A) can not produce depression (C). Rejection and failure can not produce feelings of worthlessness. However, if a person overgeneralizes a rejection and begins to believe, *"Because Kathy doesn't love me I am completely unlovable,"* depression will likely follow such an erroneous belief.

CORRELATES OF IRRATIONAL BELIEFS

At this point, we need to recognize that grieving the loss of a loved one is not considered unhealthy. On the contrary, doing so is entirely healthy. However, if four years after a loss a person is still despondent, then one may consider the possibility of an irrational belief keeping the unhappiness alive.

The three major correlates of irrational beliefs focus on

1. negative view of self,

2. negative view of the world or,

3. negative view of the future (Beck & Shaw, 1977).

Typical irrational ideas that are held for each of these core beliefs are as follows:

1. Negative view of self

   "I'm a no good piece of shit."

   "I can't do anything right (therefore I'm worthless)."

   "I'll never be good enough."

2. Negative view of the world

   "Life sucks!"

   "The world is an awful place."

   "Life is too hard. It's awful."

3. Negative view of future

   "It'll only get worse."

   "Things won't ever be any better than they are right now."

   "The world's so screwed up, it's going to end."

OVERGENERALIZATION

Depressed patients tend to overgeneralize in their thought processes. This is especially true of teenagers who have a tendency to think crookedly anyway. They have a tendency to believe that because something happened once, it's going to "always" happen. A possible way to dispute this is by pointing out that any idea that supports the notion that we "know" what's going to happen in the future is irrational. No one, not even a 16 year old, has a crystal ball.

Ch 6   Depression   57

Bob: *I know I'll flunk history, I did last semester, too. Then I'll have to take summer school and I won't have time to spend with Dorothy and she'll dump me.*

Therapist: *Just because you flunked history once doesn't mean you'll flunk it again does it?*

C: *No . . . but I will. Just wait.*

T: *Bob, you may be right. I'll promise you one thing; if you keep telling yourself "I'll flunk, I'll flunk" you're making it harder to get a passing grade.*

Another common theme in this type of irrationality is the idea that because *"no one seems to value me now, no one ever will"* or because *"things are bad now, they will always be bad."* You can challenge this by explaining that no one can tell the future. More importantly, you are making predictions about how people will treat you that may not have even been born yet. What could be crazier than that?

PERSONALIZING EXPERIENCES

Depressive clients tend to overpersonalize their experiences. They pick out small pieces of information and ignore data that will not support their perceived worthlessness.

Carrie: *The principal said, "You freshman better grow up." I think he was talking to me.*

This can be quite frustrating when you have a small mountain of objective data that suggests otherwise, but the student refuses to focus on any data other than the small amount that supposedly supports the worthlessness.

EMBRACING THE NEGATIVE

Depressed students tend to embrace the negative. This may be particularly frustrating to a classroom teacher who

58   Rational Counseling With School Aged Populations

doesn't understand the dynamics of the situation. Complimenting a child who has an internalized "tape" that plays *"I'm a rotten person"* will produce cognitive dissonance or a mild form of anxiety. The child is telling self *"I'm rotten"* and a teacher says *"You're a fine young person."* Obviously, this is confusing.

At this point the child can either (1) change his/her self-perceptions of or (2) act in a way to reaffirm his/her badness. Unfortunately, the latter of these two options typically is the one taken.

A teacher once told me, *"It seems like whenever I compliment him, he turns around and does something really mean."* She was quite accurate with this judgment by my observations.

What can be done? These are TC's (tough customers), but you can have successes by actively and continuously challenging their badness. Where is the evidence that you are a bad person? There are no rotten people, just people who act rottenly.

TECHNIQUES

Bad 100% Technique

A technique I use quite often with such children is designed to get the clients to realize that to be "bad," 100% of your behavior must be bad. Try taking a piece of paper and draw a large circle. I'll ask the client, *"What percentage (or part) of your behavior is bad?"* They may say a figure such as 50%, which is probably an overestimation of their bad behavior. Then draw a line through the circle to designate the "bad" behavior. Then ask, *"What percentage (or part) of your behavior is good?"* Again, draw a line through the circle to designate the "good" behavior. At this point I usually state, *"Well, the rest of your behavior must be neutral which means not good or bad."* You can then use the drawing to explain that the child is a lot like you (the therapist); you do some good things, some bad things, and some things that are in the middle. This simple technique can have a dramatic effect, especially on younger clients such as six to eight year olds. I usually follow up with an idea like this:

> "We've shown right here on the paper that you're not a bad person. You're like everyone else. It wouldn't make any sense to keep telling yourself you're no good when we've just proven that that's not true. That's like believing the world is made of green cheese. You don't believe that ,too, do you?"

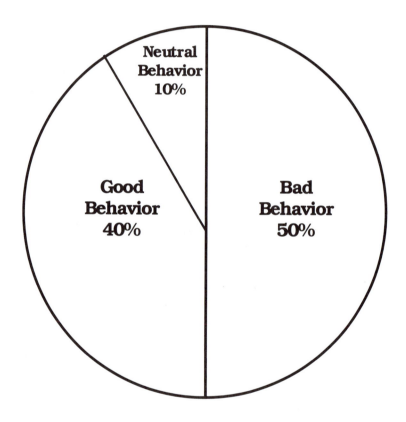

Figure 6.1. A technique to remind children not to confuse their behavior with their "value as a person."

Challenge the C Technique

Ellis and others have made the point that you always have an option regarding where to start with irrational beliefs. You can challenge the "A" such as:

> C: *Nobody loves me.*
>
> T: *That's just not true. Your parents put a roof over your head, feed you, clothe you, take care of you, live in a house where you have your own room . . . that's a lot of caring and concern for parents who don't love you.*

The more elegant way to tackle such a problem is to take the student's situation or thinking to the logical (or illogical) extreme.

> C: *Nobody loves me.*
>
> T: *Let's assume that you're right for a minute, and nobody loves you. Why would that be a fate worse than death? Worse than being boiled in hot oil? Couldn't you get at least a little bit of enjoyment out of life anyway?*

Flat Tire Technique

Howard Young (1977), in his excellent chapter, suggested the flat tire example to help teach teenagers not to overgeneralize bad behavior into bad personhood. Ask the client if he/she would "junk" a whole car if the only thing wrong was a flat tire. When he/she says "no," it is a good opportunity to point out that he/she is "junking" himself/herself when he/she puts self down for mistakes.

Eliminate the Irrational Technique

A good example can be drawn from sessions with a 16-year-old Navajo female. Mita came to see me due to feelings of worthlessness. Concentrating was hard for her and I believed she was experiencing enough uncomfortableness that she would work hard in therapy.

Many of our early sessions were spent working on basic concepts of rational versus irrational and trying to get her to focus on her self-talk. As we moved along, the problem became clearer. She had been reared in a dysfunctional home and had continually been verbally abused. She had been told, *"You're stupid, you're ugly, and you'll never amount to anything."* For the past decade this charming little girl had been reliving those painful memories and reindoctrinating herself almost daily. The behavioral problems initially consisted of peer relationship problems and academic problems but over the past couple of years things had gotten worse. Why had things gotten worse? Because she had gotten better at cutting herself down.

Many times with clients like this, you can use your relationship to an advantage. I told the client I thought I was an excellent judge of character and I did not believe she was stupid, ugly, or a nobody. Also, what her parents or I thought didn't matter. Instead what she thought about herself was what really mattered. I pointed out how her thinking was "doing her in" and she was good at understanding this logic. She did make gains and even asked a boy to the prom which was surprising to everyone. However, she was still haunted by "the tapes."

Breaking the Cycle Technique

One final technique I use with depressed clients (and other clients as well) has to do with breaking the cycle of depressive thinking. I find many depressed clients have a tendency to ruminate in their depression. They shut themselves off from other people and spend an excessive amount of time alone, pitying themselves.

I tell clients when they are sitting around downing themselves that it is best to break this pattern. They should try to imagine a scene that is totally the opposite of what they're feeling when depressed and think of a funny scene or thought. The goal is to get the student to replace his/

her self-downing with any other thought—hopefully a thought that will promote his/her sense of well being.

This is not in any way, shape, or form a cure. It is a simple technique to help kids feel better momentarily and break out of the depressive cycle.

64 Rational Counseling With School Aged Populations

CHAPTER **7**

SELF-ESTEEM

As stated earlier in this book, **low self-esteem** usually is the result of being overly concerned with others' opinions of you. Most treatment strategies focus on the cessation of self-rating or the tendency to judge your inherent value by the goodness of your deeds. **Individuals who excessively self-rate and require others' approval tend to lack assertiveness.** The reason for this is fairly obvious. If they were to stand up for what they believe in, it would mean risking being disapproved which is usually too great a risk for the neurotic.

Another important goal of therapy is to get clients to accept themselves without demanding that they be any more than they happen to be. I've read magazine articles that state that over 90% of American women are displeased with their appearance. Less than 10% of the women in this country can look in the mirror and feel at ease with their appearance.

These individuals tend to be very insecure. To keep their feelings of self-worth, they not only must keep individuals' approval today, but also must be concerned about tomorrow. These poor folks tend to act like hamsters on an exercise wheel; the faster they run the faster they have to keep running. The only way to win at this game is to step off the wheel. This can be a difficult task. Such thinking is usually deeply ingrained and has been reinforced by this culture for many, many years.

Ch 7   Self-Esteem   65

Therapist: *Why does it matter what your brother thinks of you, Francine?*

Francine: *Well, I really look up to him. I want him to approve of what I do.*

T: *You know what? I think it's more than wanting him to approve. I think it's more like "He has to approve or I'm a shit."*

C: *Maybe.*

T: *Do you see that once you turn it from a preference of "I'd like him to be happy with me, but I'm not gonna sweat it because I can't control it" to an absolute requirement to survive, that you are really setting yourself up to be miserable?*

C: *Why?*

T: *Because you are demanding control over something you can't control. You'll spend a lot of energy worrying and fretting about it.*

Another case was with a 17-year-old female who was continually dieting although she was of average size and weight.

Therapist: *So how are you doing today?*

Mary Jane: *Terrible, I gained two pounds this weekend.*

T: *Mary Jane, you really are concerned about your weight aren't you? I always thought you were kidding about wanting to lose weight but you're serious.*

C: *Why shouldn't I be? I'm up to 108 pounds.*

T: *What does it prove about you that you weigh 108 pounds?*

66   *Rational Counseling With School Aged Populations*

C: *That I'm fat.*

T: *O.K., what would it mean if you were fat?*

C: *That nobody would be my friend. No guys would want to date me and I'd be miserable.*

I wish I could describe some simple technique, but usually I've found that you spend a lot of time just hammering away at the core irrational idea, *"I need others' approval to feel O.K. about myself."* In this instance, a helpful procedure might be to distinguish with your clients between a "want" and a "need." Many clients confuse these two concepts.

Therapist: *Rhona, can you tell me what it means to really need something?*

Rhona: *Well, it would mean you have to have it.*

T: *You have to have it or what would happen?*

C: *You'd be really disappointed.*

T: *No, without a need you would be dead. A need is something you have to have to live. Can you give me a few examples.*

C: *You mean like food and water?*

T: *That's right, food, water, shelter, air to breathe. Sometimes we call things we want, needs. We say things like, "I need that new sweater" or "I need to be popular." Do you see what I mean?*

C: *Yes, I think I see.*

T: *What I'm try to show you is that when you turn a "want" into a "need" you're playing with fire. Let me give you an example. If I said, "I need to have milk in the refrigerator at all times. Without it I'll die." How would I feel*

Ch 7   Self-Esteem   67

> *if I opened up the refrigerator and there was no milk?*

C: *Like you were going to die, I guess.*

T: *Right. Now what if I thought, "I'd like to have milk in the refrigerator but it's not a big deal if I don't. I want it, but I don't have to have it." Now I look and it's gone. How will I feel?*

C: *Not as bad. You'd probably stay pretty calm about it.*

T: *That's right. Good.*

Low self-esteem can manifest itself in a wide variety of behaviors. Individuals with low self-esteem will not typically be risk takers. They have the skills to complete a project or task but can not "pull the trigger." They blame others for their current life situation, but the truth is that they typically have been too hesitant to take advantage of a situation that presents itself. Again, if you absolutely require certainty before you'll take a step out on a project, you won't be stepping out very far. As far as modern science has determined, death and taxes are the only certainties on which you can totally rely.

LOVE SLOBS

A very common subclass of low self-esteemers is a group of individuals Ellis has referred to as "love slobs" (LS). This is a common problem especially among high-school-aged students. My experience has been that females are more likely to suffer from love slobbism than males, but I have seen absolutely no clinical studies on this subject.

As the name implies, love slobs are desperately seeking love and approval. They are the type of individuals who are continually bouncing from boyfriend to boyfriend or girlfriend to girlfriend. It is almost as if without love and approval they will die. LS tend to hold onto an irrational idea that closely mirrors that sentiment . . . *"Without someone to love me, approve of me, and value me, I am completely unlovable."*

LS seem to always be in a state of crisis. When they have someone to feed their neurotic need for acceptance, they are terrified of losing this person. When they don't have someone, they are even more miserable because they perceive this "singleness" as proof of their worthlessness.

I predict that in the future an increase in love slobs will occur because the conditions that produce them do not appear to be on the decline. As was stated earlier in this book, from the time children are old enough to understand language, they are bombarded with the message that *"you are not inherently acceptable and lovable. To become acceptable and lovable you must look a certain way, act a certain way, and be a certain way."* Individuals learn that they have to attempt to earn or acquire their worth, and what better way than to have a special someone to continually tell you in words and actions that *"you are lovable."*

INTERVENTION TECHNIQUE

An intervention that I have found to be useful is **shame attacking.** The parallel between the concept of shame and love slobbism is important. A shameful person is embarrassed or ashamed, not by what they do, but by who they are. They believe they are inherently less than adequate, much like the love slob. Encourage love slobs to come to school looking somewhat disheveled (hair undone, unattractive clothes). They are to concentrate on not feeling terribly uncomfortable. The rational statements might look something like this:

> ***Rational statement:*** Too bad if I look like a mess. It is certainly not a catastrophe if others dislike the way I look. That's their problem. Even if they talk bad about me, it's just words, it won't kill me!

Love slobs always seem to be concerned that they are performing adequately or look acceptable. Many times these are the teenagers who "sleep around." They will give their bodies to receive the attention they desire out of this perceived need. As has been said before, these individuals usually take considerable effort but one bright spot does exist. Many LS are quite unhappy and are tired of "running in the wheel" as it were. They can be motivated easily and are ready to give up these destructive ideas.

CHAPTER **8**

ANXIETY

Before discussing anxiety a beneficial procedure would be to discuss briefly the difference between anxiety and fear. Bard (1980) described **anxiety** as an emotional response which humans experience when they perceive dangers that seem real to them but which are mainly imaginary because so little probability of occurrence exists. On the other hand, **fear** is an emotional response to the threat of harm or injury.

RET tries to distinguish between these two on the basis of the underlying beliefs that produce each emotion. For example, the child who believes that he/she cannot go on the swings because something bad might happen, and he/she couldn't stand the pain if he/she did fall, is actually making the swings seem more dangerous than they really are. Many children fall off the swings and live to tell the tale. This child is giving up a great deal of possible enjoyment. The child who does not want to go to school because older children are physically assaulting him/her is slightly different. The threat of harm is more real and not imagined in this situation. However, such situations usually vary by degree. An important step is to determine whether the fear is appropriate, given the situation, or if it is exaggerated and out of proportion.

The core irrational belief that usually accompanies anxiety is that the feared event (for example, speaking in front of the class) will be terrible, awful, and catastrophic. The belief is an exaggeration of some event's "badness." A typical ABC analysis of an anxiety would look something like this:

Ch 8   Anxiety   71

A—Speaking in front of the class

B—"I might make a fool of myself and that would be terrible—a fate worse than death."

C—Anxiety

WAYS OF DISTORTING ANXIETY

As you may know, children and teenagers are great at "awfulizing" or exaggerating something from bad to terrible. They commit errors of inference (Grieger & Boyd, 1983) which can be any number of ways of distorting reality. Typically, one observes the following:

1. overgeneralization—believing that because they were anxious regarding an event at one time, they will behave inappropriately again.

2. selective abstracting—placing emphasis on a portion of the information while ignoring all information that does not support their irrational, anxiety-provoking idea.

3. maximizing—or awfulizing and exaggerating something's badness.

DISCOMFORT ANXIETY

Ellis (1962) differentiated between **ego anxiety** and **discomfort anxiety** in which a child's comfort or security is threatened. Again, the threat does not actually cause anxiety. The child's awfulizing or catastrophizing about the threat does. In discomfort anxiety, look for irrational ideas similar to the following:

"I must not feel threatened."

"It is terrible that bad things happen."

72   *Rational Counseling With School Aged Populations*

"If something bad may happen I must be preoccupied with it."

"I can't stand it when that happens."

Anxiety can be difficult to identify with some children because they do not exhibit clear, anxiety-like symptoms. When you find a child who has learned to cope by avoiding a certain situation, a reasonable possibility is that the child is anxious regarding some stimulus in that environment.

Additionally, certain physical conditions can produce anxious behavior. Medications can cause side effects which can produce anxiety in children. Impulsive children can look anxious and vice versa. As a school psychologist, I see many children each year who were referred for an evaluation due to impulsive, acting-out behavior. Many of these children appear to be suffering from attention-deficit hyperactivity disorder, but after careful analysis of the data, they are actually suffering from some type of anxiety disorder. For example, a child who is anxious and fearful of his/her alcoholic parents may very well act like a hyperactive child due to thoughts continually running through his/her head making it impossible to concentrate. These children are basically "stressed out" due to their dysfunctional home and are plagued by concerns for their safety. A student once described it to me as *"a symphony in my head,"* meaning he had more thoughts than he could attend. The ones he ignored usually came from his teacher.

As has been detailed throughout this book, RET is a cognitive-behavioral form of psychotherapy. Both cognitive and behavioral (not to mention emotive) interventions can be used.

Cognitively, RET is vital to get children to see that their thinking is causing the anxiety. They are best served if they can be given a new way to react to a feared situation. Working through the A,B,C analysis may be quite helpful in this regard. At other times, they are still struggling with their situation even after all the careful disputation. At that point, an advisable procedure may be simply to tell them what to think to keep

Ch 8 Anxiety 73

from upsetting themselves. This is not recommended in place of helping them work through their own crooked thinking, but at times it may be necessary. Children become so overwhelmed with anxiety that they have lost the capacity to sort through things independently. Here is an example of an A, B, and C analysis:

Therapist: *When do you start to feel so nervous and uptight?*

Client: *Right when I start to think about giving the speech.*

T: *That's interesting. Let me guess at something . . . once you start giving the speech you aren't nervous anymore.*

C: *Not really, no.*

T: *Why do you think that's the case?*

C: *I guess it's because once I get up there, I realize it's not that bad.*

T: *Exactly . . . what do you think you're saying to yourself before you get started?*

C: *I think that I'm going to forget what I was going to say.*

T: *And that would be . . .*

C: *That would be terrible.*

T: *That would be terrible because . . .*

C: *That would be terrible because I'd look like a complete idiot.*

T: *So at "A" you think about giving the speech. At "C" you feel very anxious. And we've just discovered the belief at "B" that was causing*

74   *Rational Counseling With School Aged Populations*

*the anxiety . . . "I might forget what I was
going to say and that would be terrible because
I'd look like an idiot."*

BEHAVIORAL TECHNIQUES

Token Reinforcement Technique

Behavioral techniques include the use of a reinforcement
schedule. A token economy, one in which a child receives
a token to be used toward a certain goal (such as a movie
rental or extended curfew), can be a nice technique that can
be used in conjunction with other cognitive techniques.

For example, I recall a seven-year-old school phobic who
had a difficult time separating from her mother. A program
was implemented that allowed the child to receive a token
if she could leave for school without begging and pleading
to stay home. When she had ten tokens she could pick out
a new doll. Within a week the child had faced the anxiety
of school and found out that she liked her teacher and was
fitting in nicely with her peers. As would be expected, most
phobias disappear rather quickly once your clients face their
fears.

Emotive Technique

Emotive techniques can be used by replacing the words
terrible and awful with the word catastrophe.

> C: *That would be terrible if my mom and dad
> got a divorce.*
>
> T: *I'll agree that it would be bad. We can name
> some bad things that would probably happen
> . . . You might have to move. You might have
> to change schools. Your mom and dad would
> not be together anymore, but I wonder if it
> would be as terrible as you think.*
>
> C: *It would be the worst thing I can think of.*

Ch 8 Anxiety 75

T: *Boy, it would be a real catastrophe, wouldn't it? As bad as an earthquake or tidal wave.*

C: *Not that bad.*

T: *Well, those are the only things I can think of that are catastrophes. Do you see how you're making your parents' divorce as bad as a catastrophe?*

C: *Not really.*

T: *What percentage of bad would it be?*

C: *I don't know . . . maybe 99% bad.*

T: *You see, but you're talking about it like its 150% bad. Like it's worse than the worst thing imaginable. How do you think you'd feel if you said to yourself, "This is bad but only bad not a terrible, awful catastrophe?"*

C: *I'd probably feel better.*

Prescribing the Symptom Technique

Another technique is called prescribing the symptom. A ten-year-old child was being treated by a fellow RET therapist. The presenting problem was the boy's germ anxiety. He would ask his mother, *"Are you sure there are no germs in my milk?"* Sometimes he would refuse to sit on the couch because he was afraid the couch was germ infested.

The therapist had the parents prescribe the symptom by saying things like, *"I'm not 100% sure you can safely sit down there. It is possible that there are germs on that couch."* The child's anxiety provoked questioning diminished. He began to get the message that such questioning was excessive and unnecessary.

76   *Rational Counseling With School Aged Populations*

Rational-Emotive Imagery Technique

An excellent technique to use with anxiety is Rational-Emotive Imagery. This technique has been explained previously and will not be discussed in detail here. The reason for this technique's relevance with anxiety-ridden individuals is that it allows a child to visually and mentally experience the feared situation. Behaviorists' theory predicts the more a person experiences an anxiety provoking situation and does not experience any noxious stimulation, the less anxious they will be during the next encounter. This reasoning is what allows REI to be so effective.

Assuming Worse Anxieties Are Realized Technique

As has been discussed earlier, RET encourages the search for elegant solutions. This technique requires assuming your worst anxieties have been realized and nothing is left to do but face the situation. It tries to get the client to realize that even when the feared event does take place it certainly is not the end of the world. Using the previous example, let's examine how this technique might be employed.

> T: *So if your parents did get a divorce, why would that be so terrible that you couldn't stand it?*
>
> C: *Because I wouldn't be happy.*
>
> T: *So you always have to be happy . . . there can be no pain in your life?*
>
> C: *I just wouldn't like it.*
>
> T: *But let's assume it does happen. Would you die?*
>
> C: *No . . . but I'd be unhappy.*
>
> T: *Why? Wouldn't it be possible to enjoy life at least a little even if this does happen.*

C: *I guess so.*

T: *What I want you to examine is your own thinking that goes something like, "I couldn't stand it if my parents got divorced." That's nonsense. Of course you could stand it, what choice would you have.*

C: *None really.*

T: *That's right. So why make things worse by believing if your parents got a divorce you could never be happy again?*

CHAPTER **9**

ANGER

RET differs from other schools of therapy in its views of anger. RET hypothesizes that anger is not caused by frustration. Anger is caused by the DEMAND that one not be frustrated. This absolute, rigidly held belief is what actually causes anger.

A typical A,B,C analysis of anger might look something like this:

> A—Parents refuse to let Lee Ann attend the homecoming dance
>
> B—*"They shouldn't tell me what to do . . . they've got no right to try and control me."*
>
> C—Anger
>
> D—*"They can tell me what to do . . . I don't have to like it. You can't get what you want just because you want it."*
>
> E—Disappointment, irritation

Ellis (1973) drew a distinction between healthy and unhealthy anger. **Healthy anger** is moderate in its intensity and includes such feeling such as irritation, disappointment, and displeasure (Bernard & Joyce, 1984.) Such emotions are

Ch 9   Anger   79

viewed as healthy because these emotions often motivate clients to change their current situation. Emotions such as rage, hate, and bitterness are considered **unhealthy** because they are usually not helpful. When one is extremely angry or enraged, he/she does not think well because the arousal of the limbic system precludes higher level functions from mediating behavior (Luria, 1973.) Think back in your life of all the really idiotic things you've done. How many were done when you were having an intense period of anger? Have you ever said anything while angry you regret later? Of course, we all have.

Physiologically, anger produces higher blood pressure, increased heart rate, and stomach difficulties (Ellis & Harper, 1975.) All in all, anger is very seldom of any practical value and definitely has negative consequences.

In working with teenage clients, one need not be surprised to find that very few understand the concept that other people and things do not make them angry. They do not realize that they make themselves angry by the way in which they think about things. To some, believing that they have an option other than immediately becoming angry is inconceivable.

TECHNIQUES

Disputing Irrational Commandment Technique

I think a helpful explanation is that when you become angry, you are relinquishing control of yourself. It is no different from the temper tantrum that a five year old pitches at the first bit of frustration. When you anger yourself, you are setting up absolute commandments for the universe and then damning people when they do not submit to your rules. The problem with setting up these rules is that other people may not agree to comply with these rules. For example, a very common irrational idea held by teenagers is, *"No one has the right to talk bad about me."* Of course, as you know, teenagers will talk badly about other teenagers. Just like the rest of us, teenagers are entirely fallible and will use poor judgment at times. By holding the commandment that

80   Rational Counseling With School Aged Populations

"Thou shalt not talk bad about me," you are almost guaranteeing that you will be angry and disappointed.

This irrational belief can be disputed in a number of ways. If the student is of reasonable intelligence, he/she has heard of and may remember some of the information contained in the Constitution. I point out to the person that one of the basic rights of every American is freedom of speech. What that really means is that we are free to say what we believe. If someone believes you're full of hot air, they have the constitutional right to say "You're full of hot air." You always have the right to ignore them. To demand that they not have the right to say what they said is un-American.

Also, even if it wasn't a constitutionally guaranteed right, they would still have the right to say what they want. Even if they were acting stupidly and cruelly, people have the right to act as such. To demand that they not have this right is like taking away their humanness. I ask my client how he/she would feel if someone took away the chances to learn from mistakes and demanded that he/she be perfect. When the person answers that he/she wouldn't like it at all, I try to get the child or young person to see that by demanding someone act differently, then that person is being stripped of his/her humanness. Now who is being unfair?

Attacking Musturbating Technique

Ellis referred to anger producing thoughts as "musturbating" or believing that things MUST be a certain way. He also described what he called "the tyranny of the shoulds" in which people believe that people and things "should" turn out better than they have.

A common way to attack such thinking is to simply ask for evidence for these beliefs. For example:

        C: *People shouldn't spread rumors like that.*

        T: *Where's the evidence for that?*

        C: *I don't know . . . they just shouldn't.*

T: *Well, for someone to spread rumors, they have to first think up a rumor, and second tell other people the rumor. Now in your case, did both of those things happen?*

C: *Yes.*

T: *Well then of course people should spread rumors because the two things that needed to happen to spread this rumor DID happen. You know what I'd like you to try to do?*

C: *What?*

T: *Stop "shoulding" on yourself. You're turning into a real musturbator.*

C: (Laughing) *Musturbator!*

T: *Yes, listen to yourself . . . people must not do this and they must not do that . . . musturbation!*

Give Up Your Anger Technique

I also encourage clients to "give up" their anger because what they are actually doing is letting another person control how they feel. If this person is someone they don't particularly care for, it is twice as bad because now they are letting this person control them when he/she is not even around. Many times an analogy can be drawn between your client and a puppet. *"You're acting like your teacher totally controls you, like you're some kind of a puppet. Don't you think it is time to cut those strings instead of letting him control you?"*

Losing My Temper Technique

Sometimes individuals talk about having "a bad temper, just like my dad." They treat the idea of a temper like it is an actual thing that crawls on their back and they can't possibly control this "thing."

82   *Rational Counseling With School Aged Populations*

Try looking around the floor like you are trying to find something.

Client: *Are you looking for something?*

Therapist: *Yes, my temper. I lost it a while ago.*

C: *Your temper?*

T: *I lost it about the time I stopped demanding the world treat me fairly. I was tired of waiting for the world to change so I decided to change. Now I miss my temper.*

C: *You miss it?*

T: *Yeah, I miss feeling very tense and angry several times a day. I miss having to apologize for what I said. I miss my stomach churning and not being able to sleep well at night.*

C: *I get your point.*

T: *Sound like anyone you know?*

C: *Me.*

T: *What do you say we work on teaching you how not to make yourself angry?*

84   Rational Counseling With School Aged Populations

CHAPTER **10**

LOW FRUSTRATION TOLERANCE

Some theorists believe that anger results from Low Frustration Tolerance (LFT) (Wessler & Wessler, 1980). While I would agree that people who have LFT also tend to become angry easier than other individuals, I also believe LFT leads to numerous other problems such as academic underachievement, social problems, and life difficulties in general.

I believe the single most important factor in predicting personal success is frustration tolerance. Since most things in life that are valuable take time, having LFT many times does not allow an individual the required self-discipline to complete an important task. Just when the going gets tough and no immediate satisfaction is in sight, you'll see the LFT'ers bail out. They end up settling in life and this pattern becomes hard to break.

The major irrational belief in LFT is "Life should always be easy and without frustration." Of course, life is not easy and contains a great deal of frustration. As Ellis is fond of pointing out, life is actually spelled H-A-S-S-L-E.

I believe that special education populations contain a higher than normal amount of LFT students. Many learning-disabled students give up on academics. They have found working quickly and simply finishing an assignment is easier than to taking the time to do it correctly. The goal is to finish, not to learn a new skill. No wonder they have a hard time academically with this attitude, coupled with the learning difficulties. What used to be one problem (learning/processing deficits) is now two problems (also LFT).

Many teenage and adult alcoholics suffer from LFT. A detailed analysis of substance abuse issues will follow, but LFT is a component of recovery that requires attention if a student is to get and stay straight.

Many times school-aged alcoholics begin drinking to medicate themselves and never learn to face difficulties of living in today's world. As some therapists in the substance abuse field have stated, they never learn to walk through the pain. Their coping skills consist primarily of drinking, drugging, denying and projecting blame onto others. They haven't seemed to learn that sometimes in life you are faced with a painful situation, and the most adaptive, healthy thing to do is genuinely experience the sadness or loss. Their LFT and accompanying beliefs have allowed them to ignore or at least avoid this process.

LFT can take many forms in school aged children (Knaus, 1983.) When you observe the following behaviors, be aware that LFT may be a primary or contributing factor:

1. Whining

2. Complaining

3. Day-dreaming

4. Lack of responsibility

5. Withdrawal or shyness

Knaus (1983) made the point that many common childhood disorders such as eating disorders, impulse control problems, compulsive disorder, anxiety disorder, and conduct disorders all can have one thing in common: low frustration tolerance. Like other compulsions, many times eating disorders result

86   Rational Counseling With School Aged Populations

from children believing they can not stand to do without things they desire. Conduct problems also have a LFT component because many of these children believe "it's too hard being good." Therefore, they believe it is acceptable to act whichever way they have an impulse to respond.

LFT can be a difficult problem because many times avoiding a frustrating task can be momentarily rewarding. On a hot day, the 13-year-old boy decides it would be too hot to mow the lawn, so he decides to go to the swimming pool instead. For the time being he is reinforced, but his inability to delay gratification will do him in eventually.

Therein lies another reason LFT is difficult to treat: No immediate punishment or negative reinforcement occurs as a result of the poor decision making. If any negative consequences do follow (such as groundings), frequently they occur days or weeks later.

TECHNIQUES FOR LFT

Disputation Technique

Disputation techniques typically focus on challenging the belief that, *"Life is too hard and should be totally free from frustration."* To dispute along these lines may be appropriate.

> **Disputation:** Where is it written that because you don't like something, you don't have to do it? Even the President does things he doesn't like . . . that's part of life.

Usually, if you trace back avoidant behavior you can examine the negative consequences of such behavior. Many times clients choose not to focus on these consequences.

> Therapist: *Milton . . . remember how you decided to not work on your science project until the very last minute and then you didn't have time to finish it?*

Client: *Yes, I remember. I got an "F" on the project and was ineligible to play baseball in the spring.*

T: *Was it worth it . . . just to go to that movie instead of working on your project?*

C: *Are you kidding . . . that movie stunk anyway.*

T: *Do you see where you're heading right now with this situation?*

C: *Yes, I suppose I really don't want that to happen again.*

Forceful Dialogue Technique

LFT children also can be taught forceful dialogue to encourage them to stay with frustrating tasks. An impulsive child who hurries through his/her homework can be taught to sub-vocally rehearse, "The slower I go, the more I know" as a self-modifying phrase.

Parameter Establishment (Timer) Technique

An experiment I ran in a Chapter 1 (remedial) math class with the help of my wife, Polly, focused on setting up parameters to encourage slower work pace. My wife continually told me, *"It's not that they don't know how to do it. They just rush through their work to finish."*

A timer was used and students were told they would have, for example, 15 minutes during which they had to work on their assignment. If the entire class worked, they would earn points toward free time on Friday. Whenever possible, if you can set up a scenario where peers monitor each other's behavior, I highly recommend it. This approach teaches them responsibility for themselves rather than having an external source (a teacher) controlling reinforcement and punishment.

The class' daily assignment grades increased dramatically over the control groups. Additionally, they improved on the weekly quizzes. A simple procedure like this helped teach

88   Rational Counseling With School Aged Populations

frustration management to groups of students who had little self-discipline.

UNDERACHIEVEMENT TECHNIQUES

Bard and Fisher (1983) defined academic underachievement as "very poor academic performance resulting mainly from students' beliefs that are false and incompatible with the objectives of the system." Underachievement does not include dyslexia and learning disabilities or other conditions that would explain the failure to perform. Bard and Fisher hypothesized a number of irrational beliefs related to underachievement:

1. Things will turn out OK whether I work or not.

2. Everything should be entertaining and/or enjoyable, and no unpleasantness whatsoever should occur.

3. To do well in school would betray the relationships I have with my friends.

4. To cooperate with authority in any way is demeaning, dishonorable, and destructive of my personal integrity.

5. Nothing I do at school will ever benefit me.

You may have noticed that beliefs 1 and 2 appear to have LFT components. Again, underachievement may be caused by simple avoidance anxiety.

Targeting and Disputing Beliefs Technique

Bard and Fisher (1983) recommended that you simply ask the client which one of the above statements is particularly accurate when it comes to describing their beliefs. When beliefs are targeted, then they can be disputed.

Time Parameter Technique

Parents can also use the timer in a similar manner as was described previously.

Behavioral Contract Technique

A wise procedure is to set up some type of behavioral contract detailing what is expected from the school. As always, parents control a majority of the reinforcers such as the telephone, television, car, and curfew that can be used advantageously.

Cognitive Self-talk Technique

A behavior program alone would miss the cognitive self-talk that is obviously affecting this problem. By now, the previously mentioned irrational beliefs should be easy fodder to pick apart. Happy hunting!

CHAPTER **11**

ALCOHOL AND DRUG ADDICTION

Quayle (1983) estimated the economic cost of alcohol and other drug abuse to be 70 billion dollars a year. Absenteeism, increased costs of health care, and declining productivity factor were estimated into this staggering figure. The human cost may be much higher.

Estimates report that from six to ten million individuals have alcohol problems (Brandsma, 1980.) Given the effect alcohol has on friends, family, and significant others, the belief is that addiction could be negatively affecting as many as 70 million Americans (Franks, 1985.)

An agreed upon definition of alcoholism has never been easily reached, as this is a hotly debated topic within the field. In DSM-III-R (American Psychiatric Association, 1987), alcohol abuse is described as repeated use of alcohol despite mounting practical problems. Alcoholics Anonymous (AA) has held a basic definition that points to problem drinking when such behavior causes the drinker's life to become "unmanageable."

RET encourages counselors to view alcoholism along a continuum with attention being paid to frequency, severity, and duration of the problem. Ellis, McInerney, DiGuiseppe, and Yeager (1988) believed that earlier AA literature described

Ch 11   Alcohol and Drug Addiction   91

alcoholism "like a disease" and over the years this metaphor has been interpreted literally. Ellis et al. (1988) stated

> it is probably equally as inaccurate to view alcoholics as helpless victims of an insidious disease as it is to view them as unenlightened and sometimes uncooperative sufferers of deficits in moral character. (p. 14)

The etiology of alcoholism is clouded in much the same way as the definition. Evidence of a genetic predisposition has been found in several twin studies (Royce, 1981; Valliant, 1983). Other researchers have focused on familial patterns of alcohol use, the individual's self-control, belief system, and history with alcohol.

A wide range of factors clearly contributes to substance abuse. A single cause probably will never be identified. A combination of biological, sociological, economic, and psychological factors all compound the difficulties caused by addiction (Greenwood, 1985).

Ellis et al. (1988) postulated that alcoholism is not the result of personality problems, but that personality problems result from alcoholism. I would like to make the point that by the time a teenager or child with a drinking problem arrives for group or individual counseling, they ARE having emotional difficulties. Emotional difficulties are a factor which one must consider during treatment whether they are the result of active substance abuse or preexisting.

What kind of emotional difficulties were most common among alcohol and drug abuser? Stating types is very difficult because several patterns seem to exist.

Many of the children and teenagers suffer from low frustration tolerance (LFT). As described earlier, they hang onto the belief that "Life should be easy and without frustration." Many of the students had developed a pattern of avoiding life's difficulties by using chemicals.

Along with LFT, quite a few students lacked the ability to judge the consequences of their actions. Having stated that, I realize that many, many teenagers have a difficult time judging the consequences of an act. However, addicted teenagers have even more difficulty in this regard.

A good number of substance abusers are prone to suffer from symptom stress. This means that they are anxious, depressed, angry, or upset regarding their addiction. They "can't stand the thought that they can't drink" which leads to anxiety. They believe "life shouldn't be so hard . . . it's not fair" which leads to anger. They truly believe that their addiction "proves what a worthless shit I am" which leads to depression. An ABC analysis of this situation may be helpful.

A. Student abuses substances

B. *"What a worthless person I am. I'll never amount to anything other than a drunk."*

C. Hopelessness, worthlessness

Alcoholics tend to judge themselves harshly and have a tendency to "beat themselves up" for their behavior. They expect perfection in themselves and others and damn themselves, others, and the world in general when it disappoints them.

Many students absolutely refuse to take responsibility for their behavior. I do not feel totally comfortable discussing alcoholism as a "disease" because I am concerned that some students will act as if they have a "reason" for being addicted. Such information, which could be selectively abstracted to serve a specific purpose, could provide an excuse to relinquish all willful control of their behavior.

RET endorses "responsible hedonism" which encourages individuals to act in a way to maximize their long term enjoyment. In living for the moment, many of these addicted students ignore the long term social, academic, and legal consequences of their actions.

TREATMENT AND TECHNIQUES

RET focuses on the irrational thinking that contributes to addictive behavior. Some theorists who prescribe to the medical model believe that since some information is supportive of a genetic predisposition, then a cognitive behavioral approach such as RET would be unnecessary and ineffective.

RET holds that predisposition does not produce hopelessness but lends support to the idea that greater effort may be effective in overcoming the problem. All behaviors appear to be multiply determined and clients with a history of alcoholism should maximize psychosocial and situational factors (Ellis et al. 1988).

Once a student is in treatment for alcoholism an important procedure is to make the seriousness of the problem clear to him or her. In groups what is continually stated is that alcoholics wind up in one of three situations:

1. recovering and working daily to keep straight,

2. in a lock-up facility like a prison, or

3. dead.

Research has supported that approximately 20% of problem drinkers will remit without treatment (Valliant, 1983.) Without treatment of serious drinking problems, the results were fatal in many cases (Valliant, 1983).

When treating the alcoholic's irrational ideas regarding drinking, the important focus needs to be on problem identification, goal setting, and assessment.

Problem Identification

Problem identification at first may seem to be obvious and even unnecessary, but many times it is an important part of the overall treatment. Denial is such a big part of addicts' coping mechanism. Many times they will not admit that they have a drinking problem. Even though they have nearly flunked out of school, are excessively absent on Friday and Monday (Friday to start drinking, Monday because they are too sick to come to school), and have DUI charges pending. They may still look you in the eyes and say *"My drinking isn't the problem. My parents are the problem."*

Challenging the Logic Technique

A helpful method I heard from a colleague goes something like this:

Therapist: *Dan, you've got 12 missed days of school this quarter. You have been picked up for driving under the influence, and admittedly you drink nearly everyday, but you want to talk about your parents! That is like someone coming to me who is on fire and saying I want to talk about this bruise on my arm. I'm not worried about being on fire. I can deal with that on my own. Do you realize how crazy that sounds?*

Goal Setting Technique

Setting goals is also important. I have met some problem drinkers who can drink occasionally without returning to problem drinking. I still find this dangerous. Some theorists believe that these individuals were never true alcoholics. Whatever the case, I find that many of the teenagers have problems with impulse control. I seriously question these clients' abilities to drink responsibly. I recall a 16 year old who described his addiction to me.

Client: *It's like once I start, I can't stop. Other guys go to a party and have two or three, but if I start, I keep drinking until the beer's gone or I pass out.*

For this reason, I encourage the goal of total abstinence. Other theorists and counselors may disagree with this, but I can only speak from my experience.

Assessment Technique

Assessment is important in narrowing the focus to allow disputation of the core irrational beliefs. When working with a student who has LFT, an advisable procedure is to either orally ask or have a worksheet of common irrational ideas that accompany LFT such as common irrational thoughts in LFT leading to Alcoholism:

- I can not survive without alcohol.

- I can't stand the frustration of not drinking.

- Life is not worth living if I can't have everything I want.

- I'm too weak to withstand the temptation.

- It is terrible that I am trying to abstain. (Ellis et al., 1988)

Another important area to assess is if a student sees drinking as an appropriate means of coping. Do they view it as terrible when they are upset? This is another way of stating they have never learned to walk through pain. Common themes are the following:

- I can't stand being upset.

- I must be happy.

- I must not be upset.

- I'm too weak to stand this upsetting emotion. (Ellis et al., 1988)

Compounding factors in alcoholism are the feelings of low self-esteem and depression that accompany problem drinking. Such feelings make not drinking more difficult, especially if the student has a habit of using drugs and alcohol as a coping mechanism.

Some of the common beliefs in this area are the following:

- Because I have an addiction, it proves I'm worthless.

- Because I'm so worthless, I drink.

96   Rational Counseling With School Aged Populations

- I have to drink to cover up my worthlessness.

- I'm such a shit. I deserve this.

Once your assessment is completed and your goals and problems are clearly identified, the real disputation can begin. The best way to start the therapy is as you would with a depressed or anxious client. As in all other forms of RET, the focus is on the client's self-talk that lead to indulgence.

**Differentiating Between Want
and Need Technique**

Many times helpful procedure is to focus on the difference between a "want" and a "need." Here is another example of how this concept can be explained.

Therapist: *How would you feel if you thought, "I want to have it be sunny today? If it's not, that would be bad but not a catastrophe." You look outside and it's raining. How would you feel?*

Client: *Well, not happy but not too bad.*

T: *You could stand it raining, right?*

C: *Yes. I wouldn't be thrilled but I could stand it.*

T: *Now, let's say you were thinking to yourself, "It needs to be sunny. If it's not, it would be a catastrophe." You look out and it's raining.*

C: *I'd feel terrible.*

T: *Now, you look out and it is finally sunny. You'd still probably feel uptight. Can you figure out why?*

C: *Would it be because it might start raining again?*

T: *Yes, that's right. Can you see how this example relates to your drinking? By thinking, "I need to drink, I have to have a drink," you're making it seem like a huge problem if you don't. What would be more true would be, "I want a drink. I don't have to have one. And since I only want one, I can definitely live without one. Nobody gets everything they want."*

C: *I see what you mean.*

T: *Try to change that need into a want. A want can be reasoned with. A need can't. Besides, drinking alcohol is only a want, not a need.*

Recognizing Choice Exists Technique

An important procedure is to work clearly through the idea that they are still CHOOSING to drink or take drugs. Many addicted clients believe that having a drug problem means, by definition, that you no longer have a choice whether or not to use. The truth may be that addicts no longer have much of a choice of how they will be feeling physically. In all likelihood, the addict will be feeling poorly without his/her daily supply. However, the student still has the choice to choose to feel poorly. Some addicts do not believe this is an option.

When this occurs, I try to point out to them that they really have no evidence that they can't feel uncomfortable.

C: *I couldn't take that because to go through that would be really tough.*

T: *Let me ask you something. Have you ever been in pain before?*

C: *Sure.*

T: *Did you stand it?*

C: *Not very well.*

98   *Rational Counseling With School Aged Populations*

T: *I didn't ask if you stood it well. I just asked if you stood it, meaning did you live through it?*

C: *Yes, I lived through it.*

T: *Another question . . . have you ever been hit in the balls?*

C: *(Laughing) Yes.*

T: *Hurts like hell doesn't it? Which would hurt more, getting hit in the balls or going without drinking for a day?*

C: *I think getting hit in the balls is about the worst pain there is.*

T: *And you stood that too. What I'm trying to get you to see is that not drinking for a period of time would not be the worst thing ever or even the most painful thing ever. You could choose not to drink and choose to experience the pain. That is an option I don't think you've really considered.*

Stopping Self-downing Technique

Another helpful technique is to try to stop the self-downing that accompanies drinking. As stated earlier, this leads to depression and then you have a student with a drinking problem who is also drinking to medicate self.

Therapist: *Tim, I sense in you that you're feeling depressed today.*

Client: *I guess I am.*

T: *Can you tell me what you're saying?*

C: *I'm saying, "I'm a no good piece of crap."*

T: *Why do you think that?*

C: *Because I am no good. I'm going to be a good for nothing drunk like my dad.*

T: *Boy, I certainly don't think you're a no good piece of crap. You seem to me to be more like a person who drinks too much. You know what that proves, don't you?*

C: *What, that I drink too much?*

T: *Yes, it proves you're human and that you're not perfect.*

C: *I know you're just trying to make me feel better.*

T: *I'm not trying to make you feel better. I'm trying to help you think better. You're free to believe whatever nonsense you want, even if it's not true.*

C: *What do you mean by that?*

T: *I mean you can walk around putting yourself down if you want, but in the end it's only making your life harder.*

C: *No, it isn't. How can a thought make my life harder?*

T: *Thoughts can make our lives harder. I believe thinking you're a piece of crap is going to lead to depression. Then we'll have a drinking problem and a depression problem. To me, that would be harder.*

Examining Triggers Technique

A helpful procedure is to examine the situational and emotional triggers that lead to the likelihood of substance

100   *Rational Counseling With School Aged Populations*

use. Important questions to be answered and answered are as follows:

Does the student tend to use alcohol or drugs when tired, happy, frustrated, bored, or anxious?

In what location are alcohol or drugs most often used?

Around which people do they most often wind up using the substance?

Have they ever wanted not to use but somehow did anyway?

What was that like?

Breaking Away from a Peer Group

Sometimes alcoholic students have a difficult time breaking away from a peer group that still intends on being involved in the drug culture. They are behaving as if they are saying, *"I want to have my cake and eat it, too."* Ultimately, the student will decide for himself/herself but the old motto "if you don't want to slip, don't go where it is slippery" may be sage advice. The situation is no different from having a dieting person stand around a bakery. The sight and sounds call up old images and the temptation is strong enough without the additional stimulus.

Waiting for the Want Technique

Many times, students come to you before they are really ready to quit. The basic message here is, *"I want to quit but only if it will be easy."* Often these students leave and, hopefully, return when they are ready to get straight. Sometimes the natural consequences of addiction take a long time to get the teenager to understand.

A final note on working with teenage addicts: FEAR DOESN'T WORK. I have seen many counselors try to scare students

Ch 11   Alcohol and Drug Addiction   101

straight, which virtually never works. Students have to reach a point where they want to be straight more than they want to be high. RET may facilitate or speed up this process, but until a student reaches the point where sobriety looks better than drunkenness, few treatments are effective.

CHAPTER **12**

RATIONAL-EMOTIVE THERAPY IN GROUPS

Given the increasing number of children and adolescents that are requiring professional assistance in their adjustment, one should not be surprised that a large number of counselors in both educational and private settings have been treating children in groups. Advantages of group counseling go beyond simply being able to treat several children at one time. Students also learn from the feedback they receive from other group members. Many times the effect of a counselor's input is minor when compared with the child's peer group. The group also can be very therapeutic through enabling a student to discover that others have problems very much like his/her own and they are dealing with these difficulties in a productive manner.

ORGANIZATIONAL STRUCTURE

Homogeneous Versus Heterogeneous Grouping

One of the initial decisions that has to be made is if you would like to group children on the basis of their presenting problem or some other bases. Having homogeneous groups has advantages, such as being able to spend more time thoroughly exploring a problem. Additionally, goals of the group can be more narrowly defined (Elkin, 1983).

Ch 12   Rational-Emotive Therapy in Groups   103

Heterogeneous or mixed groups have the advantage of containing children with different strengths and weaknesses. This way other children may observe more effective thinking and problem solving. Including one or two higher functioning children in a group for this reason also may be a good idea.

Number and Length of Sessions

The number and length of sessions also can be an important and difficult decision. Ages of children and adolescents in the group might be of prime importance. As a general rule, having more time than is required is better than having insufficient time. Role call and opening activities take valuable time and may crowd a lesson. Typically, eight to ten sessions are scheduled for a group. However, if after the allotted number of sessions you feel the group is still vital and growing, you can extend the group for several more weeks.

Group Size

Group size can vary depending upon the nature of the group. Impulsive, acting-out children may be more difficult to manage and four to six may be plenty. On the other hand, children with self-esteem difficulties may be much more manageable. When in doubt, you can adjust group sizes within the first two or three sessions.

Closed Versus Open Group

In some school districts, children are referred to the group process while a group is already underway. Whether a new member will be added a portion of the way through the process is a decision that might be best made by the group members. In this way, the group will have more of a feeling of control over the process and, hopefully, over their group experience. New members can be discussed and voted on after the group has had a chance to meet the individual.

Therapist Versus Co-therapist

The decision to have one group leader or co-therapists is also important. The presence of two talented, energetic

104   *Rational Counseling With School Aged Populations*

counselors really can be dynamic with each of you learning from each other. Additionally, more clients can be accommodated with co-therapists. If one of the therapists is ill or absent, the group can still be held.

However, co-therapists also can be detrimental, especially if they disagree on the important goals of the group. If you are going to co-facilitate a group, try to work with someone you trust and in whom have faith as a clinician.

The role of the therapist is quite active in RET groups especially during the initial stages of the group. This is because students at this point are still learning the basics and are not able to help the other group members dispute their irrational thinking.

Group Leadership

In some school districts, a movement exists to provide teachers with minimal amounts of training and send them out to be group counselors. This is a bad idea because group therapy is a very complicated and delicate process and can not be learned in a few hours. Many times the old expression about "a little bit of knowledge is dangerous" proves true. I also have found that some teachers have real talent in facilitating groups. However, many teachers have spent a majority of their educational career trying to gain and maintain control. Changing the pattern and not attempting to control the group is difficult.

Rules

In the past, I have found that a few simple rules are a good idea. The best procedure is to see if the group will produce them spontaneously, as they usually come up with reasonable rules.

Sample rules

1. Be on time.

2. Be a good listener (only one person speaks at a time).

3. What is said in the group, stays in the group.

4. No personal attacks.

Contract

Often the use of a simple contract with your group members is advisable. Contracts can give legitimacy to the group and reinforce the group policies. An example of a typical contract follows:

I, _____(insert name)_____, promise to follow the group policies that we have discussed. I will be on time, listen, maintain confidentiality, and respect the rights of others. I will receive ten points for on time attendance, ten points for participation, and ten points for completing homework assignments. I have the right to speak my mind in group. New members and major actions will require approval by a majority of group members. I understand the terms of this contract and sign under my own free will.

_____   _____
          name   date

Student Solution

Not all individuals are ready for psychotherapy, let alone group therapy. When making a decision regarding the appropriateness of a certain individual for a certain group, the overall development of the group must be the primary consideration. If a student is so difficult to control that he/she can jeopardize others' learning in the group, then he/she may be served more effectively individually.

Retaining Versus Expelling a Member

As a general rule of thumb, unless a student is clearly bothering other members let the person stay in the group. Despite his/her apparent disinterest one can not be certain that the person is not learning. A dynamic that comes into play fairly often is when a child is bothering others as a

106   Rational Counseling With School Aged Populations

means of changing the course of the group. This is a sign that what is being discussed is currently an important issue with the student.

ASSESSMENT TECHNIQUES

Group assessment focuses on the same basic areas as individual therapy assessment, e.g., vocabulary skills and overall rationality. A simple exercise is to have your group members state all the feeling words of which they can think and then try to explain the feeling associated with the word. Do not assume because a student is 17 years old, that he/she understands words like "anxiety" and "insecurity." Often they may behave as if they understand or may even think they understand, but don't.

Scenario Technique

Also, determining to what extent children can think is important. A good assessment technique is to describe scenarios and see if students can make a logical conclusion from the initial information.

> *Scenario:* Johnny is told to arrive home by 6:00 p.m. He shows up at 6:50. His parents are likely to be . . .

> *Scenario:* Sara tells Wendy she'd like for the two of them to play together. When Wendy comes over, Sara says she has changed her mind. Wendy is likely to feel . . .

> *Scenario:* Arnold tells his 5th grade class his father will buy the class pizza if they are nice to him. After a week of being nice to Arnold, the class learns the father has not promised to buy pizza. How are they likely to act toward Arnold?

Rational Sentence Completion Task Technique

I enjoy using a technique called the *Rational Sentence Completion Task* which can be used with children and adolescents alike. This can be a nice screening instrument and can be used prior to group starting. I prefer to use the sentence completion in a group setting. Pass out the form and give the group members time to complete the responses. Then you can take turns reading the responses by rotating in a circle. To do so is helpful because hesitant members will be required to respond. Usually this responding helps them relax and get used to the sound of their voices in the group. I have included the sentence completion in the appendix of this book. Counselors are encouraged to modify the instrument to meet their requirements.

Use of Inventory and Survey Technique

Use the *Idea Inventory* (Kassinove, Crisci, & Tiegerman, 1977) or the *Children's Survey of Rational Beliefs* (Knaus, 1974) as pre- and post-tests to understand attitude changes and the extent of these changes in group members. These instruments will be helpful in determining what lessons children are learning and where emphasis might be helpful. The *Idea Inventory* and the *Children's Survey of Rational Beliefs* also are included in the appendix.

HOMEWORK

Homework is an extremely important part of RET. To actually change cognitions and behaviors, a systematic program of practice is very important. Learning RET is no different from learning a musical instrument—the more you practice, the better you get.

I use the following story to try to emphasize the importance of homework.

Therapist: *Mark, I'm going to try to help you learn something that's going to seem hard or at least unusual at first.*

                   You've been thinking about the world in a certain way for a long time. I'm going to try to get you to change the way you think.

108   *Rational Counseling With School Aged Populations*

It's sort of like when you first learned to shoot a lay up in basketball? It was hard at first but now it is really easy and you don't even think about it. Actually you do think about it but it is so simple you aren't even aware of what you're thinking.

Learning this new type of thinking will be like trying to shoot a lay-up off the "wrong" foot. It will seem weird at first but if you practice enough the "wrong" foot will seem "right." But if you don't practice, it will always seem uncomfortable.

This basic example can also be used with scenarios such as learning to peddle a bicycle, driving a car, and numerous others.

Homework can take many shapes and forms. The following four types of homework assignments are among the more popular:

1. ***Keeping a log for a target behavior.*** Record the scenario where you became angry. What did you say to yourself? How did you calm down?

2. ***Shame attacking exercises.*** These were previously covered.

3. ***Bibliotherapy.*** I especially like Howard Young's *A Rational Counseling Primer* (1974) for this purpose. The book is short and has helpful illustrations. Have the group members read the first half and write a summary.

4. ***Write a rational limerick.***

   There once was a girl named Sue,
   She found herself feeling so blue,
   She thought "I'm no darn good"
   And was filled up with "shoulds"
   Unless she changed her thinking she'd be through.

Be creative. I also think an important aspect is for the counselor to do the homework as well. This can help group members view you in a new light. RET encourages counselors to be open about their own irrational thinking and using example from your life can be very beneficial.

As discussed earlier under the topic entitled "Contract," group members get credit for the homework they complete and can earn rewards either as a group or individuals. If you give the rewards as a group, some helpful peer pressure may be applied on noncompliant members. Working toward a pizza party or movie rental can make a significant difference in homework completion.

SPECIAL PROBLEMS IN GROUPS

Although treating children in groups has many advantages, some special problems will arise in groups. I will now list some of the more common problems and make some recommendations as to how to avoid or eliminate them.

Unequal Participation (Wessler & Wessler, 1980)

Some members don't talk enough and some members dominate a group. To help deal with the quiet members, I try always to plan at least one activity where everyone has to speak. Most students who are shy will quickly realize that nothing catastrophic happens when they open their mouths, so they get over this fear. Other times an appropriate procedure is to perform an A,B,C analysis of their unwillingness to share. Almost every time that social anxiety is at work, anxiety is keeping them quiet.

The dominant members can be somewhat difficult but I have found it best to encourage the other group members to gently confront the person. You can encourage confrontation by asking a leading question such as, *"How do you feel when Mike talks so much that others don't get a turn?"* Having another group member say to the overactive member, *"Sometimes I feel like you just want to talk about yourself and don't want*

110   Rational Counseling With School Aged Populations

to listen to our problems," can have a dramatic effect. Commonly, the dominating member of the group is not aware of it.

Off Task Behavior

Children can be difficult to control. This can be even more true when you are discussing issues that are anxiety provoking. Whenever possible, let the other group members handle the discipline and set up their own system for dealing with disruptive behavior. They are much more strict than is necessary.

If I have one student that is somewhat unruly, I will try to sit next to that student so I can monitor him/her. When necessary, a discussion of why we are here and what is expected of the student occurs. Occasionally, students are so unwilling to cooperate that they can not be effectively treated in a group setting. Allowing the group to decide what is to be done at this point is recommended.

Advice Giving (Wessler & Wessler, 1980)

Many times, students will fall into the trap of giving advice to other students which is best left ungiven. Rarely do students actually want advice. They want someone to listen and to help with their problems, but that does not include taking advice.

Typically, I confront the situation head on and remind the group that we're not here to solve everyones' problems for them. We are here to help them to gain understanding of their problems and how they are contributing to their problems with irrational thinking. Being supportive is great but being Ann Landers is not what we're after.

SAMPLE LESSONS

The following is a sample of lessons for a group counseling program. I will present an opening activity, major lesson, and closing activity for this curriculum.

Lesson 1: Welcome to the Group

Opening Activity. To help get over the initial anxiety of being in a group, a helpful procedure is to plan activities that require responses. The opening *go round* can focus on how the previous week went for each member. They can give one high point and one low point or rate their week on a scale from 1 to 10 with 1 being very bad and 10 being very good. They then can explain why their week was a "7" or "10."

Major Lesson. I like to use the first week to go over group rules and contracts. Also, a general overview of the upcoming group process can be helpful. I may explain a few basic ideas about RET, but a majority of the time is spent on fun activities.

Closing Activity. During initial sessions perform some "fun" activities to encourage participation. Also, if the activities aren't enjoyed at first, they won't be around for later.

Have the students pair up and learn three things about their partners. After they trade tasks, they come back into group and share the information.

Depending on the group, sometimes early exercises, that are mildly anxiety provoking, can be helpful. For example, on the count of three, have everyone make an animal noise of their choice. If group members can get over the idea of looking "goofy" in front of others, it can relax them and break the nervous energy.

Lesson 2: Feeling Words

Opening Activity. Have each group member write something about himself/herself on a piece of paper. Read the descriptions one at a time and try to guess who wrote each one.

Major Lesson. Have the group name as many feeling words as possible. Try to distinguish between physical sensations like pain and feelings like anger.

112   Rational Counseling With School Aged Populations

As stated earlier, make certain that children understand words and concepts before you attempt to talk about them.

At this point you can go around and say *"Would someone share a time that they felt . . . ?"* After a while, the group doesn't need to be led. This type of sharing will help with the closeness of the group as well.

Closing Activity. Do *The Knot Game.* Have the group form a circle facing each other. Reach across the circle and grab two hands (but not the same person's hands). Without unclasping hands try to untangle the knot.

Lesson 3: Thoughts and Feelings

Opening Activity. Without talking have the group members line up by age with the youngest in the front and the oldest in the back.

Major Lesson. Knaus (1974) had an excellent tool for helping establish the connection between thoughts and feelings. The Happening-Thought-Feeling-Behavior is presented in Figure 12.1.

Happening	Thought	Feeling	Behavior
Math test on Friday	"I'll never pass the test."	Panicky	Avoid studying and do poorly on the test

Figure 12.1. Happening—Thought—Feeling—Behavior Diagram.

An event is placed in the happening square.

    Happening: Math test on Friday.
    Thought: I'll never pass the test.
    Feeling: Panicky.
    Behavior: Avoid studying and do poorly on the test.

After you have walked through several examples, distribute previously prepared cards with situations on them. Have the group break up into pairs and complete one of the cards. Possible examples are as follows:

- Nelda gets dumped by her boyfriend.

- Monica is called an "idiot."

- Robert is held back in school.

- Sara is told she can't leave the house Friday night.

As you can tell, the HTFB can dove tail very nicely with the ABC model. Some counselors will present one or the other, but not both as they feel this would be confusing.

Closing Activity. Have the group think of a name for their group that somehow describes them. This can be an important part of building group cohesiveness.

Lesson 4: Rational versus Irrational

Opening Activity. Have the group members gather in a circle facing the back of the person in front of them. Try to simultaneously sit on the lap of the person behind you without falling down. No chairs are used for sitting, only laps. Good luck and try not to crush anyone!

Major Lesson. The objective is to help the group members determine the difference between rational and irrational thoughts. Such an important lesson may very well require more than one week.

Going over a handout describing the difference is helpful. Let the group members keep the hand out as a "cheat sheet" to help them. The best source I have found was written by Ellis in the front of a book called *Twenty Years of Rational Therapy* (Wolfe & Brand, 1977).

114   *Rational Counseling With School Aged Populations*

Rational versus Irrational.

A rational belief is true.

A rational belief can be proven.

A rational belief is usually stated as a wish or preference.

A rational belief leads to moderate emotions (such as regret, concern, and irritation).

An irrational belief is not true.

An irrational belief can not be proven.

An irrational belief is usually stated as a demand.

An irrational belief leads to extreme emotions (such as depression, preoccupation, or rage).

Again, providing a work sheet with several beliefs and asking students to determine which are rational is a good practice technique. Discussion among the group numbers is to be encouraged so that their thought processes and reasoning can be examined and confusing points can be cleared up.

A point that bears mentioning is that until students have mastered this skill, further progress in therapy will be limited. This does not mean that the group can not move on to other lessons to help clarify this concept.

Closing Activity. "Simon Says" is a popular childhood game in which a group of children try to follow commands given by the leader. To avoid being "put out" of the game the players must follow only the commands that are preceded by the phrase "Simon Says." The leader's task is to sometimes include the phrase "Simon Says" but other times simply give a command without the phrase. If the players follow a command without the phrase "Simon Says" preceding it, they are eliminated from that game. The last person left in the game is the winner.

Lesson 5: Anger

Opening Activity. Have each member draw his/her family engaged in some activity. Psychologists will recognize this as a projective drawing technique known as the *Kinetic Family Drawing Test* which can provide valuable data. After they are finished, have them tell the group about their drawing.

Major Lesson. The reason for using anger as the initial troublesome emotion is because most people have had a history of anger producing situations. It is a fairly straight forward lesson as opposed to self-rating which is not as clearly laid out.

Have students give you a situation in which they find it easy to anger themselves. Perform an A,B,C, analysis or a HTFB work up. An excellent homework assignment for this exercise involves having members record their anger episodes and bring them to the group. They are encouraged to use rational techniques to calm themselves, but since disputation has not been taught yet, this is usually not successful. Try it anyway to determine who has a "knack" for this type of activity.

Closing Activity. List alternative behaviors other than becoming angry or violent when frustrated. The person who can list the most earns extra credit points.

Lesson 6: Disputing

Opening Activity. Have each member tell his/her favorite animal, movie, sports star, etc. and then tell why it is the favorite.

Major Lesson. Focus on the anger episodes and cognitive disputations initially. What is helpful at this point is to think through your own personal disputations verbally.

Role-plays can be helpful in disputation as well. Assign the students various roles, with the leader's job being to verbally present the players with rational thoughts as they walk through the first practice role-play. The second role-

116   Rational Counseling With School Aged Populations

play is done without verbal input as the players work through the role-play once more.

Closing Activity. Have students list three things they want out of life and how new skills learned in this group may help them obtain these things.

Lesson 7: Rating

Opening Activity. If your feelings were the weather, what would it be like out today?

Major Lesson. The purpose of this lesson is to establish that to rate your global value as a human is harmful. Ellis (1975) once stated that THE TENDENCY TO RATE ONESELF ACCORDING TO YOUR ACHIEVEMENTS IS ONE OF THE GREATEST SICKNESSES OF MANKIND.

To illustrate this concept the use of Howard Young's (1977) *flat tire* example is helpful. One bad characteristic does not diminish a person's good qualities.

This can fit well with a discussion of overgeneralizing and why overgeneralizations are irrational. You can present a statement such as, *"I failed to make the basketball team, therefore I am a failure."* Ask the group to explain what is wrong with this logic. The correct answer is that even if you fail to accomplish a goal, you are not a failure. To be a failure you would have to have failed at every task you've ever attempted in the past and at every task you ever will attempt. Obviously, to know the outcome of a task that has not been completed is impossible.

The general goal is to get the group members to realize that no matter what they do, they are not good or bad people. They will save time and energy in their lives if they simply try to enjoy their existence. One of the ways they can eliminate a great deal of anxiety and difficulty is by stubbornly refusing to rate themselves.

Closing Activity. Have members pair up and devise a plan for spreading RET to the other individuals in their home, school, and community. Give individuals with the best plan extra credit points.

Other Lessons

Lessons on anxiety, low frustration tolerance, and other important topics usually follow these lessons. Needs of group members will determine the focus of lessons that follow. After the initial lessons have been successfully completed, presenting a range of options and letting group members choose which they want to use is often helpful. By this point, I would recommend having the students monitor their language for should, must, can't, awful, terrible, and other key words that usually signify the presence of irrational thinking. When they start pointing out your errors, you know they are well on their way towards independence.

Some groups may want to use some activities repeatedly like the **rate your week** game. Also, a **closing saying** with all the members of the group holding hands can be a nice way to leave for a week. A slightly altered version of the **Serenity prayer** can work well. ("Let me change the things I can change, accept the things I cannot, and know the difference.")

LET'S GET RATIONAL (LGR)

Let's Get Rational (Wilde, 1990) is a counseling board game that can be used with both groups and individually. It can be used with clients aged 11 through adulthood. Actually, a more accurate statement would be to say that individuals who can use abstract reasoning skills are appropriate for this game. That would include some seven year olds but leave some 13 year olds in question. Up to nine individuals can play at one time.

The game is played like most standard board games. A die is rolled and a player moves the required number of spaces and performs whatever action is requested depending upon the square on which the player lands. Approximately one-

118   Rational Counseling With School Aged Populations

half of the squares have very clear directions designed to encourage self-exposure.

- Tell the group about a conflict you had this week.

- Move to a square of your choice and follow those directions.

- Tell the person to your left one thing you've learned about him/her through this group.

- Tell the group what is most on your mind today.

- Tell the group what you would like to improve about yourself.

The four Affirmation squares (one at each corner) have a special purpose. When a player lands on an Affirmation square, the other players in the group take turns stating one positive, affirming statement about the player. Finally, the player who landed on the square makes a self-affirming statement.

Affirmation squares can have a dramatic effect on the group. The sharing of affirming statements can be a very emotional experience and can draw a group closer together in a hurry.

Two Role-play squares are included. These are designed to give players practice performing an action that is difficult for them. Some of the Role-play cards focus on the A,B,C system discussed throughout this book. Examples are as follows:

- Perform an A,B,C, and D analysis of a situation where you find it easy to make yourself angry.

- Perform an A,B,C, and D analysis of a situation where you find yourself putting yourself down because of your behavior.

Other Role-play cards require an actual role-play that was described earlier in this book. Two examples are as follows:

Ch 12   Rational-Emotive Therapy in Groups   119

- Role-play being assertive in a situation where it would be best to stand up for yourself.

- Role-play resolving a conflict with a friend or family member.

Ten squares are entitled "Rational Reminder Pick-up Cards." When a player lands on one of these squares he/she is to pick up a Rational Reminder Pick-Up Card and read aloud the card's saying. Seven examples are as follows:

- Life does not have to be better or different because you want it to be that way. You can either accept life or make yourself miserable with your own irrational thinking.

- No one likes frustration but we can darn well stand it.

- There are no "bad" people, just people who at times act badly.

- We do not run the universe; therefore, we cannot get what we want just by demanding it.

- You can make it without love. Few people like it but we all can stand it.

- Nothing in life is so bad that you can't stand it. You can make things seem worse than they really are by exaggerating the problem.

- No one ever guaranteed that life would be totally fair. Accept life's bad breaks with its good fortune.

The advantages of "Let's Get Rational" are many:

1. The game is enjoyable and counseling is attended more regularly.

2. The game format is non-threatening and encourages even the most resistant clients to "open up."

Rational Counseling With School Aged Populations

3. The forced communication of squares and cards gives people permission to share. Many so-called, "tough" kids will chatter like jay birds once they've landed on a game square. In formal therapy this would be a violation of their image but when it is in a game format, it is acceptable.

4. "Let's Get Rational" provides a great many "teachable moments." The game is merely a tool and can be used to emphasize certain points. Blank cards are included and counselors are encouraged to make up their own cards that apply to their groups.

5. "Let's Get Rational" is generic enough in its concepts that nearly any problem can be addressed through these cards. This is what some have referred to as the "horoscope effect."

   For example, a Rational Reminder Pick-up card may read "You can be your own worst enemy. No one else can make you feel worthless." I can't tell you how many times a player has read a card and it appears that the group was just discussing such a topic. It seems uncanny.

6. LGR can be used in a wide variety of groups. As of this writing, LGR is being used in the following types of groups:

   • Children of Alcoholics (To focus on their negative self-evaluations, overgeneralization from their parents' behavior to all others' behavior, and low frustration tolerance)

   • Children of Divorce (To focus on awfulizing, self-downing, rational problem solving, etc.)

   • Anger Control Groups (Self-explanatory)

   • Self-esteem groups (To focus on not rating oneself, stop self-downing, teach more rational decision making)

- Social Skills Groups (To focus on rejection, wants versus needs, awfulizing)

If you have a copy of LGR game and are using it in a unique way, let the publisher know. If you'd like to purchase a copy, write to

> LGR Productions
> 3083 Main St.
> East Troy, WI 53120

A colleague uses the game with individual clients and simply takes turns drawing from the Rational Reminder Pick-up cards and discussing the concepts.

The game is so new that as of this date no reviews have been printed. However, Albert Ellis has personally endorsed the game as follows (1991, personal communication): "A simple and enjoyable game that helps teach people some of the main elements of Rational-Emotive Therapy, which they can use with themselves and their friends."

CHAPTER **13**

RATIONAL-EMOTIVE THERAPY WITH PARENTS

Over the past decade or so an increase has occurred in the number of schools choosing to provide services directly to parents by way of support groups and parent training seminars or classes. Schools are now starting to realize that they can not educate a child effectively without examining the total child. To pretend that factors outside of school do not affect the child's learning is ridiculous. This move by school districts is an attempt to provide the child's parents with skills that will make their rearing of the child less problematic.

Hauck (1983) made the point that one reason for working with parents is to educate them regarding their child's emotional disturbance. A more important reason for working with parents is to provide stability so they can interact more effectively with their child. Hauck (1983) belief was that a child's emotional problems should be automatically considered more important than his/her parent's difficulties. In fact, he stated that parents should be calmed first, then concentrate on the child. If you are working in private practice, this may be an option to explore. For those of us working as guidance counselors and school psychologists in schools, it is much less of an option. Some schools do not offer parenting classes. Even if they do, often the case is that those families needing the help the most are the least likely to attend such activities.

No wonder parents have a difficult time rearing children in today's world. Demands and stressors in today's world are simply greater than they were in earlier eras. However, parents are no more prepared to deal with the difficulties often encountered in child rearing. The world has gotten bigger, faster, and more complex. Parenting has not had time to catch its breath. Bernard and Joyce (1984) stated that parents may contribute to their child's emotional difficulties not out of malice but out of ignorance.

> They may simply be unaware of the importance of being consistent, providing adequate structure, reinforcing desired behavior and extinguishing inappropriate behavior, employing logical consequences for misbehavior, giving children choices, setting appropriate expectations for compliant behavior, not being overly critical, punitive or blaming etc.(p. 314)

The goals of RET with parents are multidimensional. Bernard and Joyce (1984) have listed five goals as being important in working with parents:

1. Teach parents ways of conceptualizing the goals of families and the roles of family members as well as appropriate attitudes of child rearing.

2. Teach parents family relationship and child management skills which are necessary for them to accomplish the goals of families as well as to solve problems.

3. Teach parents the ABC's of emotions so that they can overcome their own problems, and as a consequence, are able to prevent them from being transmitted to their children.

4. Teach parents how to calm down so that they can deal with problems level headedly.

5. Teach parents the ABC's of childhood emotions so that they know how to teach their child who is having a problem.

124   *Rational Counseling With School Aged Populations*

BELIEFS

Now we will turn our attention to examine the type of thinking that leads to the most commonly reported conditions:

Beliefs That Lead to Depression

1. I have to be a good parent. Since I'm not, it proves I'm a worthless person.

2. If my child misbehaves often, it is awful and I am a failure as a parent (Bernard & Joyce, 1984).

3. My worth as a parent depends upon the performance of my child (Grieger & Boyd, 1983).

4. I am worthless because my child has so many problems (Woulff, 1983).

These are the parents who live vicariously through their children. The honors, awards, and accomplishments they never were able to receive are now up to the children to grasp. Their self-talk is as if they stated, "My value as a human depends upon my children."

Beliefs That Lead to Self-Blame and Pity

1. If you are not outstanding, gifted, and almost perfect in everything you do, you again are worthless. To make a mistake is not just a human quality, its a disaster. (Hauck, 1983)

2. If you are not loved and approved of by important people in your life, you are worthless. Rejection is painful and almost devastating, and you can not avoid being upset (Hauck, 1983).

3. We can not only be pained by physical things but by psychological acts as well. Words can hurt; gestures are painful; and a host of behaviors, even though not affecting us physically, certainly have to hurt us emotionally (Hauck, 1983).

Many parents love playing the martyr as well. Look for those parents in this area. Rather than modelling appropriate ways to handle conflict they resort to manipulation. This can be a very powerful tool, but controlling a child's behavior by projecting guilt is not healthy. The other problem is children get wise to these games, and these tactics aren't effective after awhile.

Beliefs That Lead to Anger

1. My child shouldn't be so difficult to help (Woulff, 1983).

2. My child must be fair to me at all times (Bernard & Joyce, 1984).

3. My child must do what I say (DiGuiseppe, 1983).

4. It is horrible, terrible, and awful when children do not do well, behave, or question or disobey their parents (Grieger & Boyd, 1983).

5. When you don't get what you think is right or what you deserve, you are experiencing a horrible and catastrophic event. The world should be fair and if you deserve justice, you should get it. (Hauck, 1983).

These parents need to be reminded that "kids will be kids." Childhood is a time when poor judgment is often the rule rather than the exception. If you demand that children act other than childlike, you will undoubtedly feel angry a good deal of the time.

Beliefs That Lead to Anxiety

1. My child must do well in everything (Bernard & Joyce, 1984).

2. It is horrible, terrible, and awful when children do not do well (Grieger & Boyd, 1983).

126   *Rational Counseling With School Aged Populations*

3. I must worry about my child at all times and help him [or her] overcome problems (Grieger & Boyd, 1983).

4. I must have the love and approval of my child at all times (Bernard & Joyce, 1983).

5. I cannot stand my child's behavior (DiGuiseppe, 1983).

6. I cannot stand it if something bad happens (Grieger & Boyd, 1983).

All parents worry to a certain extent about their children. Doing so is natural. However, some parents are so overly concerned with their child that the child is never allowed to think or do for himself/herself. Plus, the child will pick up on the parents' concern and actually state a belief that the world is a terrible, dangerous place where it is necessary to worry all the time.

Beliefs That Lead to Upset in General

1. My kids cause all my unhappiness. They must change for me to feel better (McMullin, Assafi, & Chapman, 1978).

2. One has to get upset when things go wrong (Grieger & Boyd, 1983).

3. My child can upset me (Bernard & Joyce, 1984).

4. I have little ability to control the unhappiness I am experiencing (Woulff, 1983).

Beliefs That Lead to Guilt

1. I am the sole cause of my child's problems (DiGuiseppe, 1983).

2. I could have and should have done something to prevent my child's disability (McInerney, 1983).

3. My child is being punished for my own personal inadequacy (McInerney, 1983).

I have been watching a pattern develop over the past decade that is alarming. Many times parents who get divorced suffer from guilt. They feel bad for not being able to give their children a "noi mal" upbringing, so they try to "make it up " to the child. One of the ways they make it up is by not placing any limits on the child which they believe is what the child wants. This may be what the child says he/she wants but I firmly believe children desire clear limits. For a discussion on limits as the keystone of emotional growth, see the book with that title by John Poarch (1990). These children without limits often have difficulties with impulse control and low frustration tolerance. They rarely had to delay gratification or experience frustration, so they never learned these important lessons.

Getting at these irrational beliefs is important because many times the parents' beliefs are adopted by the children. As stated earlier, a first step in helping the child is helping the parent.

ASSESSMENT

In working with parents, as with working with children assessment is an important step in the therapeutic process. Questions to be answered are as follows:

- What are the core irrational beliefs held by the parents?

- Of what self-talk are the parents aware when the child is misbehaving?

- How is the child disciplined?

- Are any preceding conditions associated with the problem behavior?

- Can the parents provide a united front?

- Do the parents themselves have emotional difficulties?

- How do the parents view their parenting styles?

- Does the child have problems in other environments or just around the parents?

- Are the parents consistent?

- Is the child using the behavior to manipulate the parents or is the behavior beyond his/her control?

INSIGHTS FOR PARENTS

Hauck (1983) defined manipulative behavior as any behavior that is goal directed. He went on to provide several insights for parents.

Insight #1

For a child to maintain a behavior he/she must be getting reinforced. If not, the behavior would extinguish. The difficult problem is to determine what exactly is reinforcing to the child.

For example, a seven-year-old boy was referred because he was being mean to his sister. The child did not appear to be a violent child, at least at school, but at home he was hitting and pushing his sister. After discussing the situation with his parents, my first thought was that the boy was acting up to get attention from his parents. His father worked long hours and was exhausted when he returned home. Often he did not spend any time with the boy. The child soon found that he immediately got attention, albeit negative attention, by hurting his sister.

Insight #2

Parents are usually the people most frequently involved in rewarding the behaviors of their children. I've said to parents a hundred times, "You control most of the good stuff like

Ch 13 Rational-Emotive Therapy With Parents 129

the phone, the T.V., the allowance, and the curfew. At school all we control is lunch and recess." As the therapist, you are responsible for helping parents understand how they are reinforcing behaviors that they want to eliminate.

Insight #3

When parents change their training methods, children change their behaviors. Hauck made an excellent point that parents often make serious errors in implementing the plans that have been discussed for their children. When the parent stops tolerating the behavior and is motivated enough to change the way they are dealing with it, then the child will begin to change. Without parent change, there will be no child change.

Insight #4

Actions speak louder than words. By this time, sermonizing to the child in all likelihood will be a waste of time. An advisable procedure is to give the child a choice when he/she will not listen to your requests. For example, "if you want to use the phone tonight, I expect you to take out the trash." In this way, the option is clearly left up to the child. The choice is his/hers. If the child is unhappy with the choice, he/she has made (not to take out the garbage), then the child has within his/her power to change this choice and thereby gain phone privileges.

Insight #5

Guilt and pity prevent the implementation of this program. When the parent will not allow the natural consequences of the child's actions to affect the child, how is the child to learn? As stated earlier, this rescuing behavior has at its base selfishness, pure and simple. The parents are actually minimizing their suffering by taking on their child's suffering. Since watching their child suffer has been deemed "too painful," they attempt to save the child from any harm. The real world doesn't work like this and, in effect, you're teaching the child to play the game with different rules. How fair and loving can that be?

130   Rational Counseling With School Aged Populations

McInerney (1983) believed that in working with parents you have a tendency to run into the same problems a fair amount of the time. Typically, a larger percentage of parents do not believe or will not admit that their child has any type of problem. The facts of the case can be disregarded or minimized.

Many parents have a hard time dealing with the anger of having a disturbed child. The self-talk in this case seems to focus on the incredible unfairness of the world and the need for the world to be just and fair. The use of all the disputation discussed in this book for anger are appropriate here.

Parents sometimes mistakenly believe that being angry with the child's principal or teachers is productive (or at least it feels good). This rarely works and usually sets up an adversarial relationship between the home and the school. The individual who usually gets hurt by this type of situation is the child.

OVERCOMING PROBLEMS

Ellis, Moseley, and Wolfe (1966) made the following recommendations from their book, *How to Raise an Emotionally Healthy, Happy Child.*

Overcoming Problems with Hostility

1. Be calm yourself. If you become easily upset, you will teach your child that to become upset when others do not act the way you want them to act is acceptable.

2. If possible, remove unnecessary frustration from the child's environment.

3. Try to minimize the amount of time your child is overly tired, cold, or physically uncomfortable.

4. Do not condemn a child when he/she has behaved badly. Instead explain that he/she has acted badly, but do not berate the child's personhood.

5. At times, a wise procedure is to let your child get the anger out of his/her system.

6. Use a diversion to distract the child so he/she can calm down.

7. When the anger is the result of your child's jealousy over the possessions of another child, then is a good time to point out that all things are not fair and equal in this world.

Overcoming Fears

1. If your child is frightened by specific things such as dogs, try to keep him or her away from those things as much as possible.

2. Keep the easily upset child out of the way of excessively fearful adults and children.

3. Train yourself as a parent not to acknowledge fear when around your child.

4. Children and adolescents can be talked out of their fears if they are reasoned with on an ongoing basis in a patient, kindly manner.

5. Teasing the child for his/her fears will only make the child feel more inadequate in handling the situation, which is why he/she probably is fearful in the first place.

6. Humor to help individuals overcome fear may be appropriate.

7. Help the child to become familiar with the feared object. Such exposure may lessen his/her fear.

8. Calmness in dealing with the child's fears is a prerequisite.

Overcoming Achievement Difficulties

1. Raise your child so that he/she can enjoy many types of achievement not only for the sake of winning, but also for the personal satisfaction.

2. Teach your child that real achievements are rarely easy.

3. Praise your child when he/she is acting in an appropriate manner. Do not confuse good behavior with good personhood.

4. Perfectionism is great as long as it relates to performance and not to your self. Nothing is disturbing about wanting to get straight A's, but believing that because you got straight A's you are more worthwhile than others is neurotic.

5. Teach your child that achievement and popularity are not the same thing, and many times may be opposite.

6. Make certain your child's preferences for achievement stay just as that . . . preferences and not needs.

134   Rational Counseling With School Aged Populations

CHAPTER **14**

RATIONAL-EMOTIVE THERAPY WITH TEACHERS

One of the biggest problems associated with teaching today is stress. Teaching has a high burnout rate, and increasing numbers of our nation's best educators are leaving the field. When these individuals are asked why they left, typically the answer is not due to the low salary. More often than not, they left because of the continual stress of the job. If you have ever been surrounded for eight hours by 20 to 30 children, you will understand!

Teaching RET to teachers makes perfect sense for the same reason it makes sense to teach RET to students. If we can provide teachers with a means of calming themselves and tools to better handle the stress they experience, they will be better able to do their job.

The goals of a stress-reduction program would be to help teachers understand where their emotions originate and how they are able to control and limit a majority of their negative emotions. To do this, an extensive amount of information regarding the association between beliefs and emotions also would have to be presented.

Ch 14   Rational-Emotive Therapy With Teachers   *135*

Bernard and Joyce (1984) defined stress as

> a function of an individual's interpretation of a situation
> as demanding or threatening, of the individual's expectation
> of being able to cope with this perceived demand or threat,
> and the individuals appraisal of both the initial perception
> of a demand or threat as well as of the personal and
> interpersonal consequences of the demand or threat."

Such a definition is largely based in cognitive terms. I prefer a simpler definition of stress which states that any demand or perceived demand on a person can be stressful.

As you certainly recognize by now, RET supports that what is important in stress is a teacher's belief about the event and not the event itself. This does not mean that certain events are not stressful, because, obviously, some are. RET still contends that a teacher has within his/her skills the ability to think rationally about a given situation and can, therefore, significantly reduce stress.

STRUCTURE

In helping teachers with negative emotions, a very appropriate approach would be to hold a teacher's support group in the school to address some of these issues.

To organize and hold such a group, one of the first steps would be to determine when would be the best time for teachers to meet. My guess would be that before school would be the most productive time because teachers, like students, do not like to stay after school. Besides, many teachers coach after school and would be unavailable. Plus, in the morning teachers are fresh and not exhausted from the day.

The use of bibliotherapy may be especially beneficial due to the educational nature of teachers' jobs. Several books would work in this capacity. The most popular of these books is *A New Guide to Rational Living* by Ellis and Harper (1975). Like other clients, teachers are uncomfortable with the idea of "group therapy." They believe only "crazy" people or people with serious problems go to group therapy. Keeping the focus

136   *Rational Counseling With School Aged Populations*

of the group as an educational group may help side-step some of these concerns.

The initial sessions could be quite formal, for example with an adolescent group where concepts are presented and discussed. Forman and Forman (1980) recommend the following sequence:

1. The Nature of RET and REE

2. The ABC's of Emotion

3. What is Rational?

4. Rational Self-Study

5. and 6. Common Irrational Ideas

7. Dealing with Anger and Hostility

8. Dealing with Fear and Anxiety

9. Dealing with Guilt

10. Building New Thought Habits

VALUE OF RET FOR TEACHERS

Why is RET useful for teachers? Paraphrasing Bernard & Joyce (1984), the answer is that RET enables teachers to solve their own personal problems so that these problems do not interfere with the teaching of children. The healthier the teacher, the more energy he/she will have to devote to the demanding job of teaching.

As teachers, these individuals are in an ideal spot to introduce the concepts of RET to their students. In this way, children are not only being educated regarding certain academic subjects but also regarding the nature of emotions.

RET can be used preventatively to keep children from becoming depressed, anxious, rage filled, and unable to tolerate frustration. As the old saying goes, "an ounce of prevention is worth a pound of cure."

RET reinforces critical thinking and independence which are both beneficial to the student in many ways. RET also promotes self-acceptance and self-reliance.

COMMON IRRATIONAL BELIEFS
OF TEACHERS

The most common irrational beliefs of teacher are much the same as the irrational beliefs of children and the rest of the public. They tend to focus around **self-worth statements, should statements,** and **awfulizing.**

I'm Terrible

Many teachers believe that they need to have complete control of their classes or they are terrible teachers. Add to this the equally illogical premise that, "if I am a terrible teacher, then I am a terrible person," and you can understand why these teachers continually are downing themselves. Some derivations of these themes are as follows:

- I have to be adequate at all times.

- If I fail as a teacher, I fail in life.

- I have to have the respect of the students.

- I must have the respect of the staff.

- When things go wrong it is my fault and that proves how thoroughly rotten I am.

- If the principal knew what really went on in here, I'd be fired.

138   Rational Counseling With School Aged Populations

These statements can be countered by rational disputations such as the following:

- Where is the evidence that I have to be adequate? Nobody is adequate all the time.

- My value as a teacher and my value as a person are two very different things.

- I would like the students and staff to respect and like me, but if they don't, I can certainly stand it.

- Even if things go very wrong, it still only means I'm capable of failing.

- Even if I were fired, I could always enjoy myself in another line of work.

As has been said before, whenever you start rating your personhood according to your accomplishments, you are asking for trouble. Unfortunately, some of the best teachers push themselves so hard because they believe their value as a person depends on how well they teach.

Children Must Be Different

Teachers, who are prone to be excessively angry and hostile, undoubtedly are demanding that the children they are teaching be different than they are. This idea is clearly irrational and typically is found in statements such as the following:

- Those students have no right to act up like that.

- They should be more respectful.

- I must not be challenged.

- Teaching shouldn't be this hard.

- Those students are rotten little kids for acting like that.

These statements can be disputed with the following rational statements:

- Of course they have a right to act up . . . after all they're just kids.

- If they were more respectful, it would be nice, but no absolute evidence exists that they should be more respectful. My desires can't make it so.

- Being challenged is not the worst thing in the world.

- They have the right to act badly due to the fact that they are fallible human beings.

- Teaching should be just as hard as it is because it is hard. My demanding that it should be easier will not change a thing.

- These students are only acting LIKE rotten little kids and are not rotten kids. No such thing as a rotten little kid exists, just little kids who act rottenly.

Things Are Awful

Teachers who have difficulties due to anxiety are probably making things worse than they seem or "awfulizing." Such beliefs manifest themselves in statements such as the following:

- Isn't the way these students act terrible?

- Keeping up with the work is too hard.

- A catastrophe occurs when students don't do what I tell them.

- The way the principal treats us is awful.

- I can't stand these students!

These beliefs can be challenged with thoughts such as the following:

140   Rational Counseling With School Aged Populations

- That these students are so difficult is unfortunate, but it hardly qualifies as a catastrophe.

- Keeping up with the work is hard, but not too hard. I can do it if I choose to.

- Misbehaving students are bad, but certainly not as bad as a natural disaster.

- The principal does treat us badly, but I can take it. Where is it written that everyone has to be fair and pleasant to me?

- I may not like the way these students are acting, but I can stand nearly anything.

APPROACHES AND OUTCOMES

All activities such as REI, active disputing, and rational voice versus irrational voice can be used in a teachers' support group. The goals are the same . . . to educate teachers as to the nature of their irrational thinking so that they can learn techniques to combat and change their crooked thinking into more realistic and rational thinking. Perhaps the greatest advantage would be that the children would be taught to think in a more rational manner throughout the day rather than just in groups. Imagine a school with the faculty, administration, and mental health professionals all working toward a common goal with the children. No telling what might be accomplished.

142   Rational Counseling With School Aged Populations

CHAPTER **15**

TRANSCRIPTION

The following is an account of a series of sessions conducted with a 14-year-old hispanic female. The student was referred to me by a teacher who reported that Maria appeared to be sad, and the teacher was concerned regarding her well being.

TRANSCRIPT OF INTERVIEW WITH MARIA

Session 1

Therapist: *It's nice to meet you. Thanks for coming down to talk to me. One of your teachers asked me if we might work together a little bit. Does that sound O.K.?*

Client: *Yes.*

T: *Your teacher said you seemed to be feeling really sad lately. Is that true?*

C: *Who told you that?*

T: *Well, I told your teacher that I wouldn't get into that with you. I don't think you have to worry about it. She was just wanting to help.*

C: *Oh . . . Whatever.*

Ch 15   Transcription   143

T: *Can you tell me what the problem seems to be?*

C: (No response)

T: *I want you to know that anything we talk about in here is going to stay in here. I promise I won't tell anyone what we talk about unless you tell me you're going to hurt yourself or someone else, then I have to tell. So can you tell me what's up?*

C: *It's my dad.*

T: (Nods head and leans forward)

C: *He's always on my case about everything.*

(Author's Note: Note the awfulizing. After this one statement, some evidence already exists that anxiety also may be a problem.)

C: *I can't seem to do anything right. Whenever something goes wrong he blames me.*

T: *What happens when something goes wrong?*

C: *He has a fit and screams his head off at me. I can't take it anymore. I swear I wish he would leave. He hates me.*

T: *Has he ever hit you?*

C: *Not for a long time.*

T: *What's a long time?*

C: *Since before he moved out when I was seven. He and my mother split up but they got back together. That was the best time of my whole life. It was just me, my mom, and my brothers.*

T: *So how often does he yell at you?*

144   *Rational Counseling With School Aged Populations*

C: Almost everyday. Sometimes more than once a day.

T: How do you feel when he's yelling at you?

C: Bad.

T: Can you explain that more? Are you feeling angry, scared, sad, or what?

C: When he's yelling, right when he's yelling I feel nervous. After, I just go to my room and try and calm down.

T: How do you feel afterwards?

C: Sort of still scared but mainly sad after a while.

T: So you're mainly scared and nervous when he's yelling but sad and depressed afterwards.

C: (Nods)

T: Are you willing to try and work with me to see if we can't make things a little easier for you? Let me clarify that. I can't make things go different in your home. What I can try to do is teach you a way to make it through these shouting episodes without feeling so upset. Does that sound like something you'd like to try for as a goal?

C: I guess so.

T: Great. Let's start with something called the ABC's. I bet you thought you already knew your ABC's didn't you? (At this point the therapist takes out a piece of paper and puts an "A" at the top.) O.K., the "A" here stands for the activating event or another way of saying it is "A" stands for what actually happened. So at "A" we'll put down "Dad yells at me." Down here we'll put "C" which stands for consequence or how you felt. We've

Ch 15   Transcription   145

already talked about the fact that when your dad is yelling you feel . . .

C: *Scared.*

T: *Right, another word for scared is anxious so down here we'll put scared and anxious. Now, most people think that "A" causes "C" or that being yelled at causes you to be scared but that's not true.*

C: *What do you mean?*

T: *Let me see if I can explain it. There's a middle part here called "B" which stands for belief that actually causes you to become anxious. Let me give you an example. You play softball after school, don't you?*

C: *Yes*

T: *Have you ever hit a long one?*

C: *Yes.*

T: *When you hit this long one, what did your teammates and people in the stands do?*

C: *They cheered and clapped.*

T: *What else do they do?*

C: *What do you mean?*

T: *Don't they tell you to run. Don't they sort of yell and scream at you to run?*

C: *Yes, I guess they do.*

T: *So all your teammates and the people in the crowd are yelling at you to run. They all yell and cheer but you don't get nervous, do you?*

146   *Rational Counseling With School Aged Populations*

C: Well I might be a little nervous, but not like when my dad yells at me.

T: O.K., now if yelling at "A" is what's making you nervous at "C," why weren't you just as nervous playing softball?

C: I'm not sure.

T: I think I know. It's because what is actually making you nervous is what you think ABOUT being yelled at, and you think two different things in those two situations. What were you thinking when you ran the bases?

C: I wasn't thinking.

T: You may not have been aware of it but you were thinking something because we think and talk to ourselves almost all the time. Sometimes we're not aware of it. I bet you were thinking, "This is great I really nailed the crap out of that one!"

C: Yeah, I guess I was thinking something like that.

T: Now what were you thinking when your dad was yelling at you.

C: I don't know for sure.

T: Could it be something like "This is terrible. It's the worst, and I absolutely can not stand it for one instant longer."

C: Maybe, I guess that is probably pretty close.

T: Now can you see how by thinking two different things here at "B" you felt two different things here at "C"?

C: Yes, but it's different.

T: *What's different?*

C: *It's different when it's really happening. I can't take it anymore.*

T: *Maria, listen. I'm not going to try and tell you that you should like being yelled at because that's crazy. That's not what I'm trying to get you to see at all. What I'm saying is maybe if we can think about this problem differently, we can handle it better. That's all.*

C: (Nods head)

T: *You said something a minute ago that I want to talk about for a little bit. You said, "I can't take it." Let me ask you something. How long has this gone on?*

C: *For a long time now, ever since I was a little girl. It's just worse now.*

T: *You see you can take it. You've been taking it for years now. I know you don't like it because no one likes to be yelled at, but you said "I can't take it." How would you feel if you said I wish he wouldn't yell at me but he probably will because he has now for the last several years? I can take it. I don't like it, but I can take it.*

C: *I probably wouldn't be as nervous.*

T: *Exactly. I promise you, if you could think that way instead of thinking here at "B," "This is terrible, awful, and I can't take it for one more minute," you'd feel much better. That's what I'm going to try and teach you . . . to listen to what you say to yourself and change the bad tapes into good tapes. O.K.?*

C: *O.K.*

148   *Rational Counseling With School Aged Populations*

T: *Now, an important part of this is what you'll do in between sessions. For next week I want you to listen to this tape and do this work sheet. It's not very hard, but it is important information. Can you do that?*

C: *Yes.*

T: *Great, can you come to see me next week at the same time, 6th period?*

C: *If you'll write me a pass.*

T: *O.K. That'll work well for me then. See you next week. Do you have any questions on anything at all?*

C: *No.*

Author's Notes

Maria and I spent another 20 minutes or so just talking about school and her family. I started the session very business-like, but I also wanted to give her the chance to share with me about other things. Rapport is important, and I didn't want her to feel like I was only interested in her problem.

Maria seemed to be willing to work in therapy, and she definitely was ready to try a new way of coping. I realize it is hard to tell from transcripts but all the behavioral data I was receiving were positive . . . she seemed bright, articulate, and motivated.

I contacted and met with Maria's father and encouraged him to consider family counseling. I even made the phone call and put him on the line to the clinic, but the family never did attend a single session. He did give permission for me to continue working with his daughter. I made it very clear that this in no way was going to address the family issues that were at the core of this problem, but he had the option of ignoring my recommendations and he did.

Session 2

T: *Maria, thanks for coming. I've been thinking about you and wondering how you're doing.*

C: *Not very good.*

T: (Nods and leans forward)

C: *My dad is still yelling at me. He blew up again last night because I was late coming home after school. He called me a "stupid idiot."*

T: *You felt how after he said that?*

C: *Really sad, like nobody loves me at all.*

T: *Let's talk a little bit about that.*

C: *O.K., but he's not going to stop yelling.*

T: *You're probably right. He's got a habit of yelling, and he's probably going to keep on yelling. Like I told you last week, we might as well focus on changing how you deal with him and try to learn not to let him upset you.*

C: *O.K.*

T: *Did you do your homework?*

C: *Yes, I've got it here somewhere.*

T: *Great, do you have any questions about this stuff?*

C: *Not really.*

T: *What does "B" stand for in the ABC's?*

C: *Belief.*

T: *What causes your feelings according to the tape?*

150   *Rational Counseling With School Aged Populations*

C: *What you think.*

T: *What you think at where?*

C: *"B."*

T: *Excellent! Now I want to try something today that I'd like you to be able to do all by yourself during the next week. So, pay close attention. I'm going to walk you through a situation where your dad yells at you so that we can find a phrase to calm yourself. Now, put your feet flat on the floor and close your eyes. Take a deep breath, and as you let it out, try to relax. Focus only on the sound of my voice and try to imagine the scene where you and your dad had your last fight. Imagine everything about it . . . what it looked like, what it smelled like, and hear exactly what your dad said to you. Try to be there in your mind. Let yourself feel nervous. When you can put yourself there in your mind, wiggle your finger to signal me.*

C: (After approximately one minute, she wiggles her index finger.)

T: *Now stay there in your mind and allow yourself to feel. Stay there a little while more.* (Pause) *Now, stay right there in your mind but try to feel less anxious. Keep hearing all the things he's saying but focus on feeling less anxious. When you get fairly calm I want you to signal me again.* (Pause)

C: *(Wiggles finger)*

T: *Alright, now slowly, take three deep breaths, and when you breathe out for the third time, open your eyes.*

C: (Opens eyes)

T: *How was that? Were you really able to feel less anxious?*

C: *Yes, I was.* (Looks sort of amazed.)

T: *O.K., here's the important part. What did you say to yourself to feel less anxious?*

C: *I said "They're just words. I can take them. This can't last forever."*

T: *Beautiful, Maria, that's great. You're really good at this. Did you really feel upset?*

C: *Yes, I almost started to cry.*

T: *Now, what I want you to do is work on doing that exact same thing at home every night. Do you have a quiet place you can practice?*

C: *My bedroom.*

T: *Good, do it just like you did it here. I'm going to write down your rational statement on this card for you. Use these thoughts to feel less anxious. What we're trying to do is to erase that old tape and put in this new tape and that's going to take practice.*

Author's Notes

The rest of the session was spent going over the concepts of rational versus irrational, so that now we could use proper terminology. We had a good session, and for the first time, I saw that she believed this RET stuff could have a very positive effect on her life.

Session 3

T: *Maria, how are you feeling this week?*

C: *Better.*

T: *If one was the lowest and 100 was the highest can you rate the last three weeks?*

152 *Rational Counseling With School Aged Populations*

C: Week 1 . . . probably a 10. Week 2 . . . maybe a 15. Today . . . maybe a 50.

T: Wow, that's quite a jump. You've been doing your homework.

C: That, and my dad hasn't been yelling this week.

T: Well, I'm glad for both of those. I want to talk a little about the in-between time when you're not getting yelled at. What do you feel like?

C: Usually pretty good, but sometimes I get depressed.

T: Now, let's do an ABC of when you feel depressed. What usually is happening when you are getting depressed?

C: I'm thinking about my family and my dad.

T: What are you thinking?

C: That they don't love me.

T: So here at "A" you are thinking "My family doesn't love me."

(Note: This is a rather unusual "A" but be clear that thinking about an event can be an "A" as it is in this case.)

C: Right.

T: Then at "C" you feel what?

C: Really depressed.

T: Now let me ask you something . . . on a scale of 1 to 100 how depressed are you?

C: Probably about a 95.

T: O.K., now, do you think a 95 is an appropriate level of depression when you think about what you are going through?

C: What do you mean?

T: Well, you are living through some tough situations right now. Your father, whom I know you love, is giving you a hard time. I expect you to be upset to a certain extent. That's natural and normal. What I want to know is does a "95" represent an appropriate level, considering what you're going through? Or could it be too high or too low?

C: I think a 95 is too high.

T: O.K., that's fine. Why don't we try to bring it down. So here at "C" we will write down depressed. Now what are you saying at "B" to make yourself feel depressed at "C"?

C: I don't know.

T: I'll give you a hint that might help. Listen to your old tapes and see if one is in there that's playing, "I'm unlovable and completely worthless." Can you hear one like that.

C: Yes, sort of.

T: What's it playing?

C: I'm no good. My own dad doesn't love me.

T: O.K., now let's talk about whether or not that's rational. Remember last week we talked about the differences between rational and irrational?

C: Yes.

T: Well, is this one rational or irrational?

154   *Rational Counseling With School Aged Populations*

C: *Probably irrational.*

T: *Correct, but why?*

C: *I don't know, but it's making me feel bad and that's why I think it's irrational.*

T: *That's good thinking and you're on target. Let's wade through this together. Prove to me that you are no good. That you have absolutely no value.*

C: *I can't.*

T: *That's right. Why can't you.*

C: *Because I do have value?* (Asks rather than states)

T: *Of course you've got value. Everyone has got value because you've got a life. You have lots of value. You'd make a good coat rack at the very least.*

C: (Laughs)

T: *You see, how else could you feel but miserable if you walk around with your "I'm no good" tape playing full blast all the time. Of course you're unhappy, because you are believing a lie. Your job or homework for next week is to write a paragraph about what we talked about in here today. Can you do that?*

C: *O.K., I think so.*

T: *Maria, you're doing a great job. Keep up the good work.*

Author's Note

We continued through several more sessions disputing the idea that she was no good. As is normal, such a belief usually starts when a child is quite young and takes a good amount of time to work through. As Ellis said, "All roads lead to shithood!" Meaning at the core of most difficulties is the deep down belief that, "I am a shit. If you really knew me, you'd know that I am thoroughly a shit because I've lived as a shit and I'll die as a shit."

Maria continued to come to counseling for several more sessions and made fine progress. She had some set backs along the way, but all in all, was motivated and did quite well.

CHAPTER **16**

FINAL NOTES

Throughout this book I have discussed the basic concepts of RET and pointed to numerous examples of how individuals needlessly upset themselves with their own irrational, unscientific thinking. As mental health professionals, we have had hundreds of hours of training and experience with these issues. We have read thousands of pages, attended seminars, and joined professional organizations to further study these issues. However, sometimes we forget to practice these lessons in our lives.

Taking good care so that we don't fall into the same demanding, rigid, and absolute thinking is important. We had best take care of ourselves so that we are able to manage the important tasks we have ahead of us.

If you are still hesitant about RET I recommend trying this "medicine" out on yourself. If you don't find yourself more accepting, more relaxed, more at peace with the world, and more alive, I'll be very surprised.

I know someone very well who is 28 years old and has no kidney functioning. He has a foot long catheter protruding from his abdomen through which toxins are removed each night through a process called dialysis. He is on a very strict diet and can not enjoy a majority of his favorite foods. He has learned to overcome his fear of needles and actually injects himself twice a week. As a result of his kidney disease, his skin itches whenever he perspires which makes being

Ch 16   Final Notes   157

in the sunlight extremely uncomfortable. Simple things like taking a walk or sleeping are now difficult. He can not father a child because of his health problems.

After all the adjustments that had to be made regarding his kidney failure, he was diagnosed with a serious liver disorder that is totally unrelated to his kidney disease. Sometime within the next few years he also will need a liver transplant. The doctors told him the chances of having these diseases at the same time (plus colitis) are so rare that they are incalculable. Yet through all this, he remains surprisingly upbeat and positive. He's not depressed and actually appears to have more of a zest for life that many others who are in perfect health. He realizes that it is unfair that he has to have such poor luck but he refuses to demand that life treat him fairly. He seems to know that this will only be a waste of time and energy. He doesn't walk around secretly raging at the cosmos, and it may sound like a cliche, but he seems to realize that each day is truly a gift. He doesn't think of what might have been. He thinks of what is. He has not lost his smile or his sense of humor. When asked how he keeps his spirits up he tells of a philosophy of life called Rational-Emotive Therapy and how it has allowed him to minimize his suffering.

I know this person quite well . . . I am he.

160   Rational Counseling With School Aged Populations

Rational Sentence Completion Task

Directions: Read the beginning of the sentence and finish the sentence in whatever manner you think is appropriate. Try to write your very first thought. No right or wrong answers exist.

I can't stand _____.

When I do things wrong _____.

I feel terrible when _____.

When something is hard for me _____.

I get angry when _____.

I worry when _____.

Difficult things make me feel _____.

Other kids think I am _____.

I feel awful when _____.

When I can't get what I want _____.

I feel sad when _____.

When I fail I think _____.

If people don't like me, I think _____.

Figure 1. Rational Sentence Completion Test.

Figure 1. Continued.

When I think about the future _____.

I am _____.

When I get treated unfairly _____.

I get nervous when _____.

I'm ashamed after I _____.

I feel like hitting something when _____.

When I do well, I think _____.

It is a tragedy when _____.

I "get down" on myself when _____.

The world is _____.

When I do poorly, I think _____.

Someday I will _____.

When I'm disciplined, I _____.

My biggest problem _____.

It is scary to _____.

I need _____.

Not to have what I want is _____.

People should be punished when _____.

Others should never _____.

The world should be _____.

Children's Survey of Rational Beliefs: Form B, Ages 7-10 (Knaus, 1974)

Directions: Next to each question there are three possible answers. Pick out the answer you think is best for you. Write the letter on the answer sheet beside the number of the question.

1. When someone calls your best friend or mother a bad name:

    a. you have to fight
    b. you have to tell him off
    c. you can think before you act

2. If you can't answer a teacher's question:

    a. you'll get a bad report card
    b. you may be able to answer the next one
    c. it shows you can't learn

3. When you get mad at somebody:

    a. it is because of what that person did
    b. you think yourself into getting angry
    c. it is because the person is no good

4. A child who throws a temper tantrum:

    a. is a spoiled kid
    b. always gets his/her own way
    c. is acting immaturely

Figure 2. Children's Survey of Rational Beliefs: Form B, Ages 7-10.

Reproduced with permission from W. Knaus (1974), *Rational-emotive education: A manual for elementary school teachers* (pp. 447-448). New York: Institute for Rational-Emotive Therapy.

Appendix   Figure 2   *163*

Figure 2. Continued.

5. You feel upset because you believe the world should be perfect. You can handle this problem by:

   a. trying to figure out why the world should be any different than it is
   b. trying to force the world to be your way
   c. telling yourself it doesn't matter how the world is

6. When you feel anxious (nervous) it is because:

   a. somebody is going to punish you
   b. you are thinking thoughts like "something awful is going to happen"
   c. you are a bad person

7. If you can't learn your school lessons right away:

   a. you'd better give up because you'll never learn right
   b. the work is too hard to do
   c. you'll need more time to practice

8. When somebody teases you, you:

   a. can wonder what his problem is
   b. think that people don't like you
   c. think that he is stupid and no good

9. If a person is not acting his age, the first thing to do is to try to:

   a. show him he is acting silly
   b. understand that not everybody act their age at all times
   c. pretend he doesn't exist

164   Rational Counseling With School Aged Populations

Figure 2. Continued.

10. When you feel worried (anxious) you:

    a.   can't stand feeling that way
    b.   think there is nothing you can do about feeling that way
    c.   can ask what you are getting yourself anxious over

11. If you have trouble learning to read that means:

    a.   you must be pretty stupid
    b.   you won't learn anything well
    c.   you have to spend more time practicing

12. The best way to get over your worries and troubles is:

    a.   try to forget them
    b.   complain to your friends
    c.   question your troubling thoughts

13. When you do well in school:

    a.   you are a good person
    b.   you know the subject
    c.   you were lucky

14. Some people who easily become angry

    a.   have a hard time liking themselves
    b.   have many bad things happen to them
    c.   can never stop being touchy people

15. A person who doesn't like himself

    a.   doesn't think much of his positive qualities
    b.   is not a very smart person
    c.   is never liked by other people

Figure 2. Continued.

16. If a person thought "It's too bad I didn't get what I wanted," he would likely feel

    a. angry (mad)
    b. disappointed
    c. nervous (anxious)

17. Your feelings come from:

    a. how people behave toward you
    b. how you think about things that happen
    c. your heart and your stomach

18. A person who is angry or "mad":

    a. has been treated unfairly
    b. sees only one side of the story
    c. is a bad person

Children's Survey of Rational Beliefs Form C, Ages 10-13 (Knaus, 1974)

Directions: Next to each question there are four possible answers. You are to pick out the answer that you believe is best for you. Write the letter on the answer sheet beside the number of the question.

1. A person who feels angry towards another person thinks:

   a. he can't stand the other person's behavior
   b. the other person has no right to act the way he does
   c. nobody is perfect and this person is no different
   d. all the above answers are correct

2. If a person states it is human to make a mistake and then feels awful when he makes a mistake, he:

   a. can't help feeling that way
   b. generally is a liar
   c. doesn't really believe it is right for him to make a mistake.
   d. will always correct his mistakes

3. A person who is angry because the world is not perfect can help get rid of this feeling by:

   a. trying to force the world to be the way he wants it
   b. telling himself that it doesn't matter how the world is
   c. questioning why the world must be the way he wants it to be
   d. giving up and pretending not to care

Figure 3. Children's Survey of Rational Beliefs: Form C, Ages 10-13.

Reproduced with permission from W. Knaus (1974), *Rational-emotive education: A manual for elementary school teachers* (pp. 448-452). New York: Institute for Rational-Emotive Therapy.

Figure 3. Continued.

4. If you see a person who is not acting his age, the first thing to do is:

   a. try to change him by teasing him out of his behavior
   b. ignore him completely
   c. tell him to grow up and act his age
   d. try to understand that everybody can act their age

5. When a person hates herself when someone laughs at her:

   a. she thinks that she needs the other person to like her so that she can like herself
   b. she has to believe that the person is unfair
   c. her grades will start to drop at school
   d. she will never get over feeling that way

6. A person who has trouble learning to read:

   a. will probably have trouble learning everything
   b. is stupid
   c. will have to work harder at it than some of his other classmates
   d. should give up because he is not going to do well

7. A person who feels annoyed when someone teases him:

   a. believes he doesn't like to be teased
   b. believes it is unbearable to be teased
   c. believes the other person should be punished
   d. always should go to the teacher for help

8. Any person who gets poorer grades in school than her friends:

   a. is going to be ashamed
   b. is not as good a person as they are
   c. can still accept herself
   d. will find that her friends will stop playing with her

Figure 3. Continued.

9. What makes a person complex?

    a. a person can have many different qualities like fairness and truthfulness
    b. a person is capable of behaving in many different ways
    c. a person is capable of thinking in different ways
    d. all of the above answers are correct

10. Which of the following is an example of a sensible (rational) belief?

    a. I don't like it when somebody is treated unfairly
    b. I can't stand it when I see somebody treated unfairly
    c. people who treat others unfairly should always be punished
    d. all of the above answers are correct

11. How would a person feel who thought "It really is too bad that I failed the test"?

    a. afraid
    b. ashamed
    c. disappointed
    d. depressed

12. If asked what they think the world is like, different people would:

    a. have the same opinion of the world
    b. agree that the world is a great planet to live on
    c. all state that the world is a complicated place
    d. have different opinions

13. Which situation can be frustrating?

    a. you put a puzzle together and find some parts missing
    b. you are not able to do what you want
    c. you can't find the meaning of an important word
    d. all of the above situations can be frustrating

Appendix   Figure 3

Figure 3. Continued.

14. A person who demands (insists) that things go his way, is most likely to feel:

    a.   angry when he doesn't get his way
    b.   good, because he is doing something to get his way
    c.   great annoyance when he doesn't get his way
    d.   both a and c are correct

15. A person's opinions are:

    a.   always based on facts
    b.   ideas about something that could either be true or false
    c.   always incorrect
    d.   based upon unsound assumptions

16. People who spend most of their time thinking how awful everything is:

    a.   usually have bad things happen to them
    b.   are usually treated unfairly
    c.   are hopeful that their life will change if they complain enough
    d.   usually solve their problems by facing them

17. Standards or values are most helpful in:

    a.   determining what personal goals to work for
    b.   know what to blame or praise yourself for
    c.   knowing who is a good person and who is a bad person
    d.   none of the above answers are correct

18. The better method of changing unsound (irrational) upsetting thinking is:

    a.   say you are going to stop thinking unsoundly
    b.   question unsound (irrational) ideas
    c.   insist to yourself that you start thinking only sound rational thoughts
    d.   try to forget your upsetting thoughts

Figure 3. Continued.

19. One thing we know about how people express feelings is:

    a. people who have had the same experiences express their feelings in the same way
    b. different people can express the same feeling in different ways
    c. all ways of expressing feelings are appropriate
    d. none of the above answers is correct

20. An example of an unsound assumption is:

    a. day and night follow each other
    b. the milk tasted sour
    c. Ann doesn't like me because her grades are higher than mine
    d. all of the above answers are correct

21. You believe something because:

    a. it is a fact
    b. it is your opinion
    c. answers a and b are correct
    d. answers a and b are both wrong

22. Most bullies have in common:

    a. they really don't like themselves
    b. they always have a lot of money
    c. they never act fairly
    d. both a and c are correct

23. A person who is angry:

    a. has been treated unfairly
    b. sees only one side of the story
    c. is a bad person
    d. all of the above answers are correct

Appendix Figure 3 171

Figure 3. Continued.

24. Someone who thinks life is awful and will never get better probably feels:

    a. angry
    b. annoyed
    c. depressed
    d. uncaring

25. Human emotions are most likely to result from:

    a. the way your parents taught you how to feel
    b. how you think about things that happen
    c. how other people think about you
    d. none of the above answers is correct

26. Everybody is likely to feel the same way:

    a. at a birthday party
    b. when they do poorly in school
    c. when they forget their best friends birthday
    d. none of the above answers is correct

27. Which of the following is not a feeling?

    a. sad
    b. itchy
    c. glad
    d. all are feelings

28. Which of the following is an example of unsound (irrational) thinking?

    a. I really don't like it when I can't play a game well
    b. it makes me sick to see her acting so silly
    c. it is too bad if I am not loved by everybody
    d. none of the above are unsound (irrational) thoughts

172   Rational Counseling With School Aged Populations

Figure 3. Continued.

29. If a person treats you unfairly, it would be appropriate for you to feel:

    a. angry
    b. good, because you think you are better than they are
    c. annoyed or sad
    d. anxious or nervous

30. A person who tries to think rationally (sensibly):

    a. never is emotioanlly upset
    b. is friendly only with people who think sensibly
    c. easily solves all his problems
    d. is better able to accept his mistakes

31. If you can accept that a bully has problems:

    a. you have to put up with his behavior
    b. you can try to change the behavior you don't like
    c. you shouldn't be upset if he or she bothers you
    d. you must stay out of his or her way

32. A person can get into emotional troubles by expecting to be:

    a. happy and comfortable
    b. successful
    c. liked by everbody
    d. all of the above answers are correct

33. Some people create extra worries and trouble by:

    a. having two problems that are difficult to solve
    b. blaming themselves for having emotional problems
    c. trying very hard and not succeeding
    d. none of the above answers is correct

Appendix   Figure 3   173

Figure 3. Continued.

34. What is a person who thinks sensibly (rationally) likely to recognize?

    a. if he is nervous he is making himself nervous
    b. if he is nervous, it is because of something that has just happened
    c. if he becomes nervous, he can't help it because he is a nervous person
    d. none of the above answers is correct

35. The best way to deal with worries and troubles is:

    a. forget them
    b. complain about them to your friends and get sympathy
    c. always solve them on your own
    d. none of the above solutions is very good

36. When you get a high score on a test, you:

    a. are a smart person
    b. know the subject well
    c. you will do well in the future
    d. were very lucky

37. A person who thinks rationally (sensibly):

    a. will sometimes feel ashamed
    b. wiil always be happy
    c. will be liked by everyone
    d. will always be successful in solving his problems

38. If you think you cna't stand being frustrated, that means you:

    a. won't have any friends
    b. really don't like yourself
    c. will never get to do things your way
    d. will probably get less work done

Answer Key to the Children's Survey of Rational Beliefs

Form B

1. c
2. b
3. b
4. c
5. a
6. b
7. c
8. a
9. b
10. c
11. c
12. c
13. b
14. a
15. a
16. b
17. b
18. b

Form C

1. b		20. c	
2. c		21. c	
3. c		22. a	
4. d		23. b	
5. a		24. c	
6. c		25. b	
7. a		26. d	
8. c		27. d	
9. d		28. b	
10. a		29. c	
11. c		30. d	
12. d		31. b	
13. d		32. d	
14. d		33. b	
15. b		34. a	
16. c		35. d	
17. a		36. b	
18. b		37. a	
19. b		38. d	

Figure 4. Answer key to the Children's Survey of Rational Beliefs for Forms B and C.

Reproduced by permission from W. Knaus (1974), *Rational-emotive education: A manual for elementary school teachers* (p. 452). New York: Institute for Rational-Emotive Therapy.

Appendix Figure 4 175

176   Rational Counseling With School Aged Populations

The Idea Inventory

(from Kassinove, Crisci, and Tiegerman, 1977)

Name _____

Sex: Male _____ Female _____

Age: _____

Date: _____

People have different ideas. We are interested in hearing about your opinions and ideas regarding the following statements. Place an "X" through the number which best reflects your beliefs about each of the ideas.

$$1 \ = \ \text{Agree (A)}$$
$$2 \ = \ \text{Uncertain (U)}$$
$$3 \ = \ \text{Disagree (D)}$$

	A	**U**	**D**
1. People need love or approval of almost everyone they consider to be important.	1	2	3
2. I feel like I'm a stupid person when I don't do as well as my friends.	1	2	3
3. Criminals need to be severely punished for their sins.	1	2	3
4. It is awful when things are not the way one wants them to be.	1	2	3

Figure 5. The Idea Inventory.

Reprinted by permission from the author, Howard Kassinove, Ph.D., Chairperson, Dept of Psychology, Hofstra University, Hempstead, NY, and *Journal of Community Psychology.*

Figure 5. Continued.

	A	U	D
5. People in my family sometimes make me very angry.	1	2	3
6. I constantly worry about dangerous accidents occurring.	1	2	3
7. It's easier to put off some responsibilities and difficulties rather than face them directly.	1	2	3
8. I get upset when there is no one to help me think about difficult problems.	1	2	3
9. It upsets me to recognize that some of my long held beliefs are almost unchangeable.	1	2	3
10. One should be upset over other peoples' problems and difficulties.	1	2	3
11. I'm afraid I won't find the one best way to deal with my superiors.	1	2	3
12. I get upset when other people dislike my looks and criticize the style of clothing I wear.	1	2	3
13. To be a worthwhile person, we should be thoroughly adequate, achieving and competent in almost all ways.	1	2	3
14. Our enemies should be made to suffer and pay for their evil acts.	1	2	3
15. I get upset and angry when my plans go wrong.	1	2	3

178   Rational Counseling With School Aged Populations

Figure 5. Continued.

	A	U	D
16. Unhappiness is caused by people or events around us and we have almost no control over it.	1	2	3
17. I frequently worry about getting a terrible disease.	1	2	3
18. I get very anxious and try to stall when I must face a difficult task like giving someone very bad news.	1	2	3
19. We need to be dependent on others and on someone stronger than ourself.	1	2	3
20. I get depressed when I realize that I'll never be able to change some of my strong habits.	1	2	3
21. I get depressed when I hear that one of my acquaintances is seriously ill.	1	2	3
22. It is awful when we can't find the right or perfect solution to our problems.	1	2	3
23. When I walk into a party, I feel very bad if people don't come over and greet me.	1	2	3
24. I feel inadequate and worthless when I fail at school or work.	1	2	3
25. People who are very bad and wicked should be blamed and punished.	1	2	3
26. I feel angry and rejected when my opinions and ideas are not accepted.	1	2	3
27. I can't help but feel depressed and rejected when others let me down.	1	2	3

Appendix   Figure 5

Figure 5. Continued.

28. When something is dangerous and causing great concern, we should constantly think about the possibility of its occurrence.　　1　2　3

29. Since I get very nervous, I avoid situations where I will have to make difficult decisions.　　1　2　3

30. I become anxious and need the help of others when I must face difficult responsibilities alone.　　1　2　3

31. Many events from our past so strongly affect us that it is impossible for us to change.　　1　2　3

32. I get overwhelmed with emotion when I see a severely retarded person.　　1　2　3

33. I worry that I won't find the right solution to my problems at school or work.　　1　2　3

BIBLIOGRAPHY

182   Rational Counseling With School Aged Populations

BIBLIOGRAPHY

American Psychiatric Association. (1987). *Diagnostic and statistical manual—revised* (3rd edition). Washington, DC: American Psychiatric Association.

Bard, J. (1980). *Rational-emotive therapy in practice.* Champaign, IL: Research Press.

Bard, J., & Fisher, H. (1983). A rational-emotive approach to underachievement. In Ellis and Bernard (Eds.), *Rational-emotive approaches to the problems of childhood.* New York: Plenuim Press.

Beck, A., & Shaw, B. (1977). Cognive approaches to depression. In A. Ellis & R. Grieger (Eds.), *Handbook of rational-emotive therapy.* New York: Springer Press.

Bernard, M., & DiGuiseppe, R. (1990). Rational-emotive therapy today. In M. Bernard and R. DiGuiseppe (Eds.), *Inside rational-emotive therapy: a critical appraisal of the theory and therapy of Albert Ellis.* San Diego: Academic Press.

Bernard, M., & Joyce, M. (1984). *Rational-emotive therapy with children and adolescents: Theory, treament strategies, preventative methods.* New York: Wiley Interscience.

Black, J. (1978). Effects of rational-emotive mental health program on poorly achieving, disruptive high school students. *Journal of Counseling Psycholology, 25,* 61-65.

Brandsma, J. (1980). *Outpatient treatment of alcoholism: A review and comparative study.* Baltimore: University Park Press.

Brody, M. (1974). *The effects of rational-emotive affective education approach on anxiety, frustration tolerance, and self-esteem with fifth grade students.* Unpublished doctoral dissertation, Temple University.

Conoley, C., Conoley, J., McConnell, J., and Kimzey, C. (1983). The effects of the ABC's of rational-emotive therapy and the empty chair technique of gestalt therapy on anger reduction. *Psychotherpy: Theory, Research, and Practice, 20,* 112-117.

DiGuiseppe, R. (1983). Rational-emotive therapy and conduct disorders. In A. Ellis and M. Bernard (Eds.), *Rational emotive approaches to the problems of childhood*. New York: Plenum Press.

DiGuiseppe, R., & Bernard, M. (1990) The application of rational-emotive theory and therapy with school aged children. *School Psychology Review*, *19* (3), 268-286.

DiGuiseppe, R., & Kassinove, H. (1976). Effects of rational-emotive mental health program on children's emotional adjustment. *Journal of Community Psychology*, *4*, 382-387.

Elkin, A. (1983). Working with children in groups. In Ellis and Bernard (Eds.) *Rational-emotive approaches to the problem of childhood*. New York: Plenum Press.

Ellis, A. (1957). Outcome of employing three techniques of psychotherapy. *Journal of Clinical Psychology*, *13*, 344-350.

Ellis, A. (1962). *Reason and emotion in psychotherapy*. Secaucus, N.J.: Citadel Press.

Ellis, A. (1973). *Humanistic psychotherapy*. New York: McGraw-Hill.

Ellis, A. (1975). *How to refuse to be angry and vindictive*. (Audio cassette). New York: Institute for Rational-Emotive therapy.

Ellis, A. (1977). Introduction. In J. Wolfe and E. Brand (Eds.), *Twenty years of rational therapy*. New York: Institute for Rational-Emotive Therapy.

Ellis, A. (1983). Working with children in groups. In A. Ellis and M. Bernard (Eds.), *Rational-emotive approaches to the problems of childhood*. New York: Plenium Press.

Ellis, A. (1985) *Overcoming resistance*. New York: Springer Press.

Ellis, A., & Bernard, M. (1985). What is rational-emotive therapy? In A. Ellis and M. Bernard (Eds.), *Clinical applications of rational-emotive therapy*. New York: Plenium Press.

Ellis, A., & Dryden, W. (1987). *The practice of rational-emotive therapy*. New York: Springer Press.

Ellis, A., & Harper, R. (1975). *A new guide to rational living*. North Hollywood, CA: Wilshire Book.

Ellis, A., McInerney, J., DiGuiseppe, R., & Yeager, R. (1988). *Rational-emotive therapy with alcoholics and substance abusers*. New York: Pergamon Press.

Ellis, A., Moseley, S., & Wolfe, J.L. (1966). *How to raise an emotionally healthy, happy child.* North Hollywood, CA: Wilshire Book.

Forman, S., & Forman B. (1980). Rational-emotive staff development. *Psychology in the schools, 15,* 400-406.

Franks, L. (1985). A new attack on alcoholism. *The New York Times* magazine, October 20, 47-67.

Gardner, P., & Oei, T. (1981). Depression and self-esteem: An investigation that used behavioral and cognitive approaches to the treatment of clinically depressed clients. *Journal of Clinical Psychology, 37,* 128-135.

Greenwood, V. (1985). RET and substance abuse. In A. Ellis and M. Bernard (Eds.), *Clinical applications of rational-emotive therapy.* New York: Plenium Press.

Grieger, R., & Boyd, J. (1983). Childhood anxieties, fears, and phobias: A cognitive-behavioral psychosituational approach. In A. Ellis and M. Bernard (Eds.), *Rational-emotive approaches to the problems of childhood.* New York: Plenium Press.

Haaga, D., & Davison, G. (1989). Outcome studies of rational-emotive therapy. In M. Bernard and R. DiGuiseppe (Eds) *Inside rational-emotive therapy: A critical appraisal of the theory and therapy of Albert Ellis.* San Diego: Academic Press.

Hauck, P. (1983). Working with parents. In A. Ellis and M. Bernard (Eds.), *Rational-emotive approaches to the problems of childhood.* New York: Plenium Press.

Heesacker, M., Hepner, P., & Rogers, M. (1982). Classics and emerging classics in counseling psychology. *Journal of Counseling Psychology, 29,* 400-405.

Hymen, S., & Warren, R. (1978). An evaluation of rational-emotive imagery as a component of rational-emotive therapy in the treatment of test anxiety. *Perceptual and Motor Skills, 46,* 847-853.

Jacobs, E. (1971). *The effects of systematic learning program for college undergraduates based on rational-emotive concepts and techniques.* Unpublished master's thesis: Florida State University.

Jarmon, D. (1972). *Differential effectiveness of rational-emotive bibliotherapy and attention placebo in the treatment of speech anxiety.* Unpublished doctoral dissertation: Southern Illinios University.

Jasnow, M. (1982). *Effects of relaxation training and rational-emotive therapy on anxiety reduction in sixth grade children.* Unpublished doctoral dissertation. Hofstra University, Hempstead, N.Y.

Kassinove, H., Crisci, R., & Tiegerman, S. (1977). Developmental trends in rational thinking: Implications for rational-emotive school mental health programs. *Journal of Community Psychology, 5,* 266-274.

Kelly, L. (1982). *Rational-emotive therapy versus Lewinsohian based approaches to the treatment of depression.* Unpublished doctoral dissertation, University of Georgia, Athens.

Knaus, W. (1974). *Rational-emotive education: A manual for elementary school teachers.* New York: Institute for Rational-Emotive Therapy.

Knaus, W. (1983). Children and low frustration tolerance. In A. Ellis and M. Bernard (Eds.), *Rational-emotive approaches to the problems of childhood.* New York: Plenium Press.

Knaus, W., & Bokor, S. (1975). The effects of rational-emotive education lessons on anxiety and self-concept in sixth-grade students. *Rational Living, 10,* 7-10.

Luria, A. (1973). *The working brain.* New York: Basic Books.

Maes, W., & Heimann, R. (1970). *The comparison of three approaches to the reduction of test anxiety in high school students.* Washington, D.C.: Office of Education.

McInerney, J. (1983). Working with the parents and teachers of exceptional children. In Ellis and Bernard (Eds.) *Rational-emotive approaches to the problems of childhood.* New York: Plenium Press.

McMullin, R., Assafi, I., & Chapman, S. (1978). *Cognitive restructing training for families.* Lakewood, CO: Counseling Research Institute.

Omizo, M., Grace Lo, F., & William, R. (1986). Rational-emotive education, self-concept, and locus of control among learning disabled students. *Journal of Humanistic Education and Development, 25,* 58-69.

Poarch, J.E. (1990). *Limits: The keystone of emotional growth.* Muncie, IN: Accelerated Development, Publishers.

Quayle, D. (1983). American productivity: the devestating effects of alcoholism and drug abuse. *American Psychologist, 38* (4), 454-458.

Rose, N. (1982). *Effects of rational-emotive education and rational-emotive imagery on the adjustment of disturbed and normal elementary school children.* Unpublished doctoral dissertation. Hofstra Unoversity, Hempstead, N.Y.

Royce, J. (1981). *Alcohol problems and alcoholism.* New York: Free press.

Trexler, L. (1977). A review of rational-emotive psychotherapy outcome studies. In J. Wolfe and E. Brand (Eds.), *Twenty years of rational therapy.* New York: Institute for Rational Living.

Valliant, G. (1983). *The natural history of alcoholism: Causes, patterns, and paths to recovery.* Cambridge, MA: Harvard University Press.

Vernon, A. (1990). The school psychologist role in preventative education: Applications of rational-emotive education. *School Psychology Review, 19,* 322-330.

Von Pohl, R. (1982). *A study to assess the effects of rational-emotive therapy with a selected group of emotionally disturbed children in day and residential treatment.* Unpublished doctoral dissertation, University of Alabama, Birmingham.

Walen, S., DiGuiseppe, R., & Wessler, R. (1980). *A practitioner's guide to rational emotive therapy.* New York: Oxford University Press.

Warren, R., Deffenbacher, J., & Brading, P. (1976). Rational-emotive therapy and reduction of test anxiety in elementary school students. *Rational Living, 11,* 26-29.

Wessler, R., & Wessler, R. (1980). *The principles and practice of rational-emotive therapy.* San Francisco: Jossey-Bass.

Wilde, J. (1990). *Let's get rational.* East Troy, WI: LGR Productions.

Wolfe, J., & Brand, E. (Eds). (1977). *Twenty years of rational therapy.* New York: Institute for Rational Living.

Woulff, N. (1983). Involving the family in the treatment of the child: a model for rational-emotive therapists. In A. Ellis & M. Bernard (Eds.), *Rational-emotive approaches to the problems of childhood.* New York: Plenium Press.

Young, H. (1974). *A rational counseling primer.* New York: Institute of Rational-Emotive Therapy.

Young, H. (1977). Counseling strategies with working class adolescents. In J. Wolfe and E. Brand (Eds.), *Twenty Years of Rational Therapy.* New York: Institute for Rational Living.

188   Rational Counseling With School Aged Populations

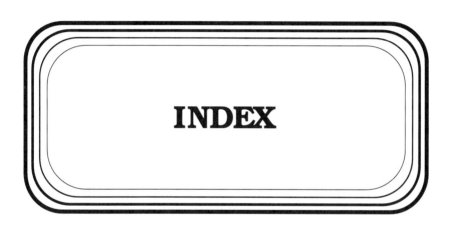

190   Rational Counseling With School Aged Populations

INDEX

A

ABC's of rational-emotive therapy 36-42
Achievement difficulties
    overcoming 133
Addiction
    alcohol 91-102
    drug 91-102
Adolescents
    behavior patterns 25-6
    concepts 25-6
Alcohol addiction 91-102
    cost 91
Alcoholics
    judgment of self 93
Alcoholics Anonymous (AA) 91
Alcoholism
    definition 91-2
    genetic predisposition 92
    problem identification 94
    techniques 95-102
    treatment 93-102
American Psychiatric Association 91, 181
Anger 42, 79-83, 116
    causes 79
    feeling 8
    produces 80
    techniques 80-3
    unhealthy 80
Anxiety 42, 71-8
    core irrational belief 71
    definition 71
    discomfort 72
    techniques 75-8
    ways of distorting 7

Argument
    responses 15
Assafi, I. 127, 184
Assertiveness
    lack of 65
Assessment
    alcoholism 95-7
    informal 31-2
    parents 128-9
    techniques for groups 107-8
    techniques for rational-emotive therapy (RET) 30-6
Aurelius, M. 1

B

Bard, J. 71, 181
Beck, A. 57, 181
Behavior
    good 60
    neutral 60
Beliefs
    children must be different 139-40
    common irrational 138-41
    correlates of irrational 56-7
    false 42-4
    I'm terrible 138-9
    irrational 10-4, 42-4
    leading to anger 126
    leading to anxiety 126-7
    leading to depression 125
    leading to guilt 127-8
    leading to self-blame and pity 125-6
    leading to upset in general 127
    rational 10, 42-4

things are awful 140-1
  true 42-4
Bernard, M. iii, v, 6, 8, 9, 35, 56,
  79, 124, 125, 126, 127, 136, 137,
  181, 182, 183, 184, 185
Bibliotherapy 109
Bill, case of 36
Black, J. 181
Bob, case of 58
Bobby, case of 27
Bokor, S. 184
Boyd, J. 72, 125, 126, 127, 183
Brading, P. 185
Brand, E. 114, 182, 184, 185
Brandsma, J. 91, 181
Braswell, L. iv, v
Brody, M. 181

C

Carrie, case of 58
Case of
  Bill 36
  Bob 58
  Bobby 27
  Carrie 58
  Dan 95
  Francene 66
  George 33-4
  Henry 47
  Hilbert 20-1
  Joan 49-50
  John 40-1
  Maria 3-4, 143-56
  Mark 108-9
  Mary 37-8
  Mary Jane 66-7
  Mike 30
  Mita 61-2
  Rhona 67-8
  Thomas 55-6
  Tim 99-100
Chapman, S. 127, 184
Checklists 35-6
  drawbacks 35
  kinds 35
Children
  working with smaller 29-30

Children's Survey of Rational Beliefs
  108, 163-75
  Answer key 35, 175
  Form B 35, 163-6
  Form C 35, 167-74
Co-therapist 104-5
Conoley, C. 181
Conoley, J. 181
Contract
  group 106

D

Dan, case of 95
Davison, G. 183
Deffenbacher, J. 185
Depression 42, 55-63
  case example 55-63
Dialogue
  forceful 52-3
DiGuiseppe, R. 5, 6, 9, 10, 14, 15,
  30, 46, 91, 92, 96, 126, 127, 181,
  182, 185
Disputation 46-53
  behavioral 50
  cognitive 46-48
  emotive 51-3
  goals of 46
  modeling of 49-50
Drug addiction 91-102
  cost 91
Dryden, W. 8, 182

E

Elkin, A. 103, 182
Ellis, A. iii, iv, v, 5, 6, 7, 8, 11,
  13, 14, 16, 23, 36, 48, 50, 52,
  72, 79, 80, 89, 91, 92, 96, 117,
  131, 136, 137, 182, 183, 184, 185
Emerson, R.W. 1
Emotions 7-8
  causes 7
Epictetus 1
Erisci, R. 35, 108, 177, 183
Experiences
  personalizing 58
Eyman, W. iii, v

192   *Rational Counseling With School Aged Populations*

F

Fear
  definition 71
  overcoming 132
Feeling
  angry 8
Feeling thermometer 34
Fisher, H. 89, 181
Flat tire 117
Forman, B. 137, 182
Forman, S. 137, 182
Francene, case of 66
Franks, L. 182

G

Gardner, P. 183
George
  case of 33-4
Gerald, M. iii, v
Goals of
  rational-emotive therapy 8
Grace Lo, F. 184
Greenwood, V. 92, 183
Greiger, R. 72, 125, 126, 127, 183
Group
  advise giving 111
  anger lesson 116
  closed 104
  contract 106
  disputing lesson 116-7
  expelling member 106-7
  feeling words lesson 112-3
  homogeneous versus heterogeneous
    103-4
  leadership 105
  length of sessions 104
  member selection 106
  number of sessions 104
  off task behavior 111
  open 104
  rating lesson 117-8
  rational versus irrational lesson
    114-5
  rational-emotive therapy (RET)
    103-22
  retaining member 106-7
  rules 105-6

sample lessons 111-8
size 104
special problems 110-1
technique 107-8
thoughts and feelings lesson
  113-4
unequal participation 110-1
welcome to lesson 112
Haaga, D. 183
Harper, G. 20
Harper, R. 80, 136, 182
Hauck, P. 123, 125, 126, 183
Heesacker, M. 6, 183
Heimann, R. 184
Henry, case of 47
Hepner, P. 6, 183
Heterogeneous grouping 103-4
Hilbert, case of 20-1
Homework 108-10
  bibliotherapy 109
  keeping a log 109
  shame attacking exercises 109
  write a rational limerick 109
Homogeneous grouping 103-4
Hostility
  overcoming problems 131-2
Hymen, S. 183

I

Idea Inventory, The 35, 108,
  177-80
Imagery
  rational-emotive 77
Insights
  parents 129-31
Intention
  paradoxical 49
Intervention techniques 69-70
Interview with Maria
  transcript 143-56

J

Jacobs, E. 183
Jarmon, D. 183
Jasnow, M. 183
Jesus Christ 1

Index   193

Joan
    case of 49-50
John
    case of 40-1
Joyce, M. iii, v, 35, 56, 79, 124, 125, 126, 127, 136, 137, 181

K

Kassinove, H. 35, 108, 177, 182, 183
Kelly, L. 183
Kendall, P.C. iv, v
Kimzey, C. 181
Knaus, W. iii, v, 35, 86, 108, 113, 163, 167, 175, 184
Knot game 113

L

Leadership
    group 105
Lessons
    group 111-8
Let's get rational (LGR) 118-22
Limerick 109
Lincoln, A. 1
Love slobs 68-9
Low frustration tolerance (LFT) 85-90
    behaviors 86
    techniques 87-90
Luria, A. 80, 184

M

Maes, W. 184
Maria, case of 3-4, 143-56
Mark, case of 108-9
Mary, case of 37-8
Mary Jane, case of 66-7
McConnell, J. 181
McCullin, R. 127, 184
McInerney, J. 91, 92, 96, 127, 128, 131, 182, 184
Mike, case of 30
Milton, case of 87-8
Mita, case of 61 2
Moseley, S. iii, v, 131, 182

N

Negative
    embracing 58-9

O

Oei, T. 183
Omizo, M. 184
Overgeneralization 57-8

P

Parents
    assessment 128-9
    insights 129-31
    rational-emotive therapy 123-33
Peale, N.V. 1
Philosophy of
    rational-emotive therapy 14-8
Play therapy 34-5
Poarch, J. 128, 184
Poll taking 51
Power-figure
    destroying 53
Practice of
    rational-emotive therapy 25-53
Problems
    overcoming 131-3
Puppets 34

Q

Quayle, D. 91, 184

R

Rapport 28-30
Rate your week game 118
Rational Sentence Completion Task 34, 107-8, 161-2
Rational therapy 6
Rational-emotive imagery (REI) 44-6, 51-2, 77
Rational-emotive therapy (RET) 123-33
    ABC's of 36-42

194   Rational Counseling With School Aged Populations

approaches with teachers 141
assessment with parents 128-9
audio cassette tape 33
cognitive-behavioral school 4
development of 5-6
goal of 38
goals 8
goals with parents 124
groups 103-22
inappropriate for 22-3
outcomes with teachers 141
philosophy of 14-8
practice of 25-53
reasons for use 19-24
structure for teachers 136-7
teachers 135-41
theory of 7-18
value for teachers 137-8
with parents 123-33
Rational-emotive therapy (RET)
  theory
      disagrees with basic client
          centered therapy 17
      disagrees with strict behavioral
          theory 16
      disputes of Freudian conclusions
          16
      emotions 14
Referred 27-8
Reinforcement 50
Relaxation
  deep 50
Rhona, case of 67-8
Rogers, M. 6, 183
Rose, N. 184
Royce, J. 92, 184
Rules
  group 105-6

S

Sample lessons 111-8
Saying, closing 118
Self
  berating 56
Self-esteem 17, 65-70
  low 65-8
  techniques 69-70
Self-referral 27-8

Serenity prayer 118
Sessions, group
  length 104
  number 104
Shakespeare, W. 1
Shame attacking exercise 52
Shaw, B. 57, 181
Spinoza 1
Stress
  symptom 23
Structure
  organizational 103-7
  rational-emotive therapy (RET)
      for teachers 136-7
Substance abuse
  factors contributing 92
  problem identification 94
  stress 93
  technique 95-102
  treatment 93-102
Symptom stress 23

T

Tape and worksheet 33
Teachers
  approaches 141
  common irrational beliefs 138-41
  rational-emotive therapy (RET)
      135-41
  structure 136-7
  value of rational-emotive therapy
      (RET) 137-8
Techniques 107-8
  anger 80-3
  assessment 95-7
  assessment in group 107-8
  assuming worse anxieties are
      realized 77-8
  attacking musturbating 81-2
  bad 59-60
  behavioral 75-8
  behavioral contract 90
  breaking the cycle 62-3
  challenge the C 61
  challenging the logic 95
  cognitive self-talk 90
  depression 59-63

Index   195

differentiating between want and
need 97-8
disputation 87-8
disputing irrational commandment
80-1
eliminate the irrational 61-2
emotive 75-6
examining triggers 100-1
flat tire 61
forceful dialogue 88
give up your anger 82
goal setting 95
group 107-8
intervention 69-70
inventory 108
low-frustation tolerance (LFT)
87-90
losing my temper 82-3
parameter establishment (timer)
88
prescribing the symptom 76
rational-emotive imagery 77
*Rational Sentence Completion
Task* 107-8
recognizing choice exists 98-9
scenario 107
self-esteem 69-70
stopping self-downing 99-100
survey 108
targeting and disputing beliefs
89
time parameter 90
token reinforcement 75
underachievement 89-90
waiting for the want 101-2
Theory of
rational-emotive therapy 7-18
Therapist 104-5
Thermometer, feeling 34
Think 8
Thomas, case of 55-6
Tiergerman, S. 35, 108, 177, 183

Tim, case of 99-100
Transcription of interview 143-56
Trexler, L. 184
Trust
establish 28-30
Tyranny of shoulds 9

U

Underachievement
techniques 89-90

V

Valliant, G. 92, 94, 184
Vernon, A. iii, v, 184
Vocabulary
lack emotional 37-8
Von Pohl, R. 185

W

Walen, S. 9, 10, 14, 15, 30, 46,
185
Warren, R. 185, 195
Wessler, R., S. 9, 10, 14, 15, 30,
46, 85, 110, 111, 185
Wilde, J. iv, 118, 185
William, R. 184
Wolfe, J. 114, 184, 185
Wolfe, J.L. iii, v, 131, 182
Worksheet and tape 33
Woulff, N. 125, 126, 127, 185

Y

Yeager, R. 91, 92, 96, 182
Young, H. 28, 61, 109, 117, 185

ABOUT
THE
AUTHOR

ABOUT THE AUTHOR

Jerry Wilde is an educational psychologist working for the East Troy School District in East Troy, Wisconsin. As a psychologist he is responsible for working with children aged three to 21 with a host of learning and emotional disabilities.

He graduated from Luther College in Decorah, Iowa in 1985 with majors in psychology and business management. While attending Luther College, he received the Omicron Delta Epsilon Award along with the Henry O. Talle Award for excellence in academic achievement. He next attended graduate school in Cedar Falls, Iowa at the University of Northern Iowa where he received his Specialist Degree (Ed.S.) in School Psychology. He is currently finishing his Ph.D. at Marquette University in Milwaukee, Wisconsin in Educational Psychology with an emphasis in Developmental Psycholinguistics. He will be completing his course work during the summer of 1992.

Recently he has invented a board game which is very much related to his expertise and professional interests. The board game, known as "Let's Get Rational," is designed to be used in a group counseling setting.

Mr. Wilde received extensive training on the use of Rational-Emotive Therapy as part of an internship while in graduate school. Since that time Jerry has been responsible for facilitating group and individual counseling programs for recovering students as well as students with a wide variety of emotional problems. Through this experience, he has refined his skills as a Rational Counselor.

Jerry and his wife, Polly, who is a graphic artist, have been married for three years. He is the youngest of five children.

About the Author   199

Other Works Available by Author

"Let's Get Rational"

A cognitive-behavioral board game designed to be used in group or individual counseling. "Let's Get Rational," teaches the basic tenets of RET to a wide range of clients with an emphasis on discovering from where "irrational" beliefs come. The game can be used with clients dealing with issues such as anger control, socialization, and recovery.

"Let's Get Rational" has been personally endorsed by Albert Ellis.

"Let's Get Rational" may be ordered from the following address:

LGR Productions
3083 Main Street
East Troy, WI 53120

Cost: $24.95 plus $2.00 shipping and handling.